NOSTRADAMUS 2

NOSTRADAMUS 2

INTO THE TWENTY-FIRST CENTURY

Jean-Charles de Fontbrune

Translated by Alexis Lykiard

HUTCHINSON
London Melbourne Sydney Auckland Johannesburg

Hutchinson & Co. (Publishers) Ltd

An imprint of the Hutchinson Publishing Group

17–21 Conway Street, London W1P 6JD

Hutchinson Publishing Group (Australia) Pty Ltd
PO Box 496, 16–22 Church Street, Hawthorne, Melbourne,
Victoria 3122

PO Box 151, Broadway, New South Wales 2007

Hutchinson Group (NZ) Ltd
32–34 View Road, PO Box 40–086, Glenfield, Auckland 10

Hutchinson Group (SA) Pty Ltd
PO Box 337, Bergvlei 2012, South Africa

First published 1984

© Editions du Rocher 1982
Translation © Hutchinson & Co. (Publishers) Ltd 1984
Set in Linotron Plantin by Input Typesetting Ltd, London

Printed and bound in Great Britain by Anchor Brendon Ltd,
Tiptree, Essex

British Library Cataloguing in Publication Data

Fontbrune, Jean-Charles de
   Nostradamus.
   2: Into the twentieth century
   1. Nostradamus. Vrayes centuries
   2. Prophecies
   I. Title   II. Nostradamus.   2. *English*
   133.3   BF1815.N8
      ISBN 0 09 158530 9

To my brother François Gurbert, artist.
To my wife Laura.
To my children Béatrice, Guillaume, Sophie and Isabelle.
To my nieces Isabelle, Véronique and Axelle.
To my nephews Alexandre, Jérôme, François Junior,
Arnaud and François-Xavier.

Letter from Henry Miller

In 1953, when I was eighteen, I had the pleasure of meeting Henry Miller, who had come to the Périgord to visit my father. I took Miller on a trip round the Lascaux caves and the Roman remains at Périgueux. These outings with one of the giants of American literature helped me to discover both the splendours of antiquity and the living heritage of the classics.

I wrote to him in 1975, letting him know I was in the process of thoroughly re-examining Nostradamus' writings. He replied on 6 June 1975 (my father had died on 6 June 1959), as follows:

Dear Jean-Charles de Fontbrune –
My reply must be brief unfortunately. About a year ago I lost the sight in my right eye. As a consequence I read and write very little. (I can only glance through the new edition you sent me.)

As for the letters, no, I do not have any of your father's letters here. Perhaps I gave them to the Library of UCLA – 405 Hillgard Ave. LA (24). Write to the Head of the Dept of Special Collections there.

I am glad to see that you are vitally interested in Nostradamus. No doubt you are an 'auteur'.

Yes, you have my permission to publish my letters to your father. Only I think you should let me look them over before printing them. I am afraid the market is glutted with books of H. M. correspondence avec [?] les un tel, [illegible] etc. etc. So pay attention!

All the best to you and to your mother if she is still alive.
    Henry Miller

PS Was this book ever translated into English[1]

---

[1] The first volume, *Nostradamus: Countdown to Apocalypse*, by Jean-Charles de Fontbrune was published in Britain on 6 June 1983.

Dear Jean Charles de Fontbrune –
My reply must be brief unfortunately. About a year ago I lost
the sight in my right eye. As a
consequence I read and write very
little. (I can only glance thru the
new edition you sent me.)
As for the letters, no, I do not
have any of your father's letters
here. Perhaps I gave them to
the library of U.C.L.A. – 405
N. Hilgard Ave. L.A. (24). Write
to the Head of the Dept. of
Special Collections there.
I am glad to see that
you are vitally inter-
ested in Nostradamus. No
doubt you are an "auteur".
, Yes, you have my per-
mission to publish my
letters to your father.
Only I think you should
let me look them over
before printing them.
I am afraid the market
is glutted with books of
H.M. Correspondence are
Le art Fel, etc. etc. So
pay attention!
All the best to you
and to your mother if
she is still alive.
Henry Miller
P.S. Was this book ever translated into English?

I
NOSTRADAMUS:
Countdown to Apocalypse (Vol. 1)
A Review of Its Readers and Critics

'In France, arsonists are left in peace,
and those who sound the alarm are persecuted.'

Chamfort (1741–94)
Thoughts and Maxims

When in 1961 I was called up for military service in Algeria, I left the
cosy comfort of Western consumer society and was plunged into a new,
often traumatic and also completely unknown world. It was like landing
on another planet altogether.

After the Second World War, during my adolescence in fact, I often
heard my father mention a future Moslem revolt in North Africa. This
was one of the main predictions he had derived from the Centuries of
Nostradamus. So I remembered his comments in 1961, the year of
General de Gaulle's 'Algeria for the Algerians', and became aware that
this was the start of a Moslem rebellion against the Christian West. By
1963, after military service, I could no longer contain the curiosity that
impelled me to check the predictions made in my father's book.

I was sorely disappointed, however. I found it dreadfully obscure:
Nostradamus's text as translated by my father remained, as far as I was
concerned, completely inaccessible.

So in my own researches I decided to start from scratch, checking the
original text and working very systematically, asking my programmer
friends to run the prophet's entire vocabulary through their computers.
I took into account both the successes and mistakes of my father's
predecessors – Bareste, Le Pelletier, Colin de Larmor, Elisée du Vignois,
the Abbé Torné-Chavigny, and the rest. I soon realized that no one had
ever really studied the minutiae of the text, which seemed to me to be
'encoded'. First of all I had to classify the key words: proper nouns,
historical and geographical names and any recurring, invented or unusual

terms. I classified all these names alphabetically, in every instance noting in which quatrain and Century they occurred.

Some years later, when I mentioned my system to a computer expert, he suggested extending such lists to cover Nostradamus' entire vocabulary, also involving a word count and an even more detailed placing and comparison of every word used. This was of invaluable assistance but could never be a substitute for an author's memory and analytical mind. To quote only one example from my filing system: I chose the word *autour*, used ten times by Nostradamus. On nine occasions the meaning was the usual one, *around* (the preposition), but once it was used in its rarer sense, as a noun meaning *goshawk*. Only when checking all ten quatrains incorporating the word *autour*, and then restoring it in context, would one be aware of the philological trap.

At last, by the end of 1979, I had arrived at an overall view of Nostradamus' 'message', along with an insight into the precision of his language and the details of his coding methods. I tried to interest several publishers without success, encountering the usual protest: 'Not *another* book on Nostradamus!' But I returned to Paris in April 1980 and saw the Business Manager of Presses de la Cité, Jean-Paul Bertrand. He was enthusiastic about my rather different, methodical approach to Nostradamus, and arranged for publication by Editions du Rocher, one of the publishing group's smaller subsidiaries.

My background is in the pharmaceutical industry and I am not a professional writer, so I was even more overjoyed. The first printing in France of *Nostradamus: Countdown to Apocalypse* was a modest run of 6,000 copies, which went on sale in the first week of November 1980. Largely through word of mouth, sales were brisk, and by late November a reprint was called for. By 10 May 1981 – the date of the French Presidential Elections – it had sold 15,000 copies. During this time the book was scarcely reviewed or even mentioned in the French press.

This silence may be explained partly by the fact that Nostradamus foretold the rise to power of the current French Socialist government, which must have disturbed some political pundits. Then as predicted, François Mitterrand swept to power on what the media dubbed 'the Socialist landslide'.

Three days later, another equally astonishing event occurred. A young Turkish fanatic tried to assassinate Pope John Paul II in St Peter's Square, Rome. In one of Nostradamus' quatrains (CII,Q97) I had discovered that the Pope's life would be in danger at such time as the Rose (Nostradamus' symbol for Socialism, and also that of the French Socialist Party) flourished in France.

These two events stimulated sudden and enormous media attention for the book, which by the end of that August had sold no fewer than

300,000 copies in France alone. Since then it has been translated and reprinted all over the world, arousing controversy wherever it has appeared.

DETRACTORS AND SUPPORTERS

'When I stop getting indignant, my
old age will have begun.'

André Gide (1869–1951)

If the various petty campaigns against my book were intended to discourage or silence me, they certainly failed. Everything I experienced in the way of journalistic hostility had all too often been encountered by more illustrious men of letters in the past, and I shall confine myself here to quoting their own words, which express far better than I could do the rational responses to unreasonable judgements and biased reviews.

Nostradamus should, appropriately, be quoted first. He himself had warned his son (see the Letter to his son César, in Vol. 1) that his prophecies would encounter hostility and derision in the years to come, and this in itself was prophetic enough. While in the important Letter to Henri, Second King of France (included here for the first time in English) he addressed this future monarch thus: 'I could have, had I wished, put a date to each quatrain; but this would not have been to everyone's liking and my interpretations would have pleased them no better, unless I had been granted enough protection to do so and had given slanderers no pretext for attacking me.'

Let us see what some thinkers and writers who came after Nostradamus have written.

'Journalists say a thing that they know isn't true,
in the hope that if they keep on saying it long
enough it *will* be true.'

Arnold Bennett (1867–1931)

'I count it one of the blessings of life that I
do not write for the newspapers. This affects my
income – but my conscience benefits from it.'

Gustave Flaubert (1821–80) *Correspondence*

'The difference between journalism and literature is that journalism is unreadable and literature is not read.'

Oscar Wilde (1854–1900)

'A libel in the newspapers is as the grass in a meadow. It springs up of its own accord. Newspapers are an especially bright green.'

Victor Hugo (1802–85) *Stone Cairns*

'Writing allows one to forget the rabble.'

Charles de Gaulle (1890–1970) *Fallen Oaks*

Now I would like to sympathize with those journalists who came to interview me after reading my book for themselves, only to find their editors censoring their copy because they had taken an independent (though not necessarily favourable) line. I remember after my lecture at the Olympia, the famous Paris theatre, on 15 February 1982, a celebrated left-wing journalist from a big daily called to see me. He had heard me talk to an audience of 1,200 people ('a few Fontbrune supporters', as another reporter claimed on the radio on the following day), and had formed his own objective, on-the-spot opinion. He certainly did not consider my statements mere sensation-seeking. The journalist I spoke to concluded our interview quite cordially, referring me to his forthcoming article. The article was definitely written but never appeared. Yes, censorship *does* exist, as all journalists well know. Here then is some food for thought for the censors:

'*Dat veniam corvis, vexat censura columbas.*'
(Censorship absolves the ravens, harasses the doves.)

Juvenal (60–140)

'Censorship of whatever sort seems monstrous to me; a thing worse than murder. An offence against thought is an attempt to assassinate the soul. The death of Socrates still weighs heavily upon the human race.'

Gustave Flaubert (1821–80) *Correspondence*

'In France every writer is on trial.'

Henri Rochefort (1830–1913) *The Lantern*

'Assassination is the extreme form of censorship.'

George Bernard Shaw (1856–1950)
The Shewing-Up of Blanco Posnet

All sorts of political labels have been unsuccessfully attributed to me. The proof of this is that I have been attacked from every political angle and by the Church too. To be predicting, in May 1980, against all the odds, the advent of Socialism (the Rose) in France, drew the wrath of the Right, while Leftists were also incensed that my book predicted the end of such a regime – then not even established. Yet right-wing indignation did nothing to prevent the change of government on 10 May 1981: history and circumstances make a mockery of the partisan views of men.

Various priests and theologians have also attacked me, usually *ad hominem*, hence (and this is actually more serious for them) many people imagine that such attacks are motivated by some anti-religious bias in my book. I must assure them that this is not the case. They could not, anyhow, speak for their Church as a whole. And when they launched their personal and ill-informed attacks they appeared to have quite forgotten such precepts as Matthew 7:1–5:

Judge not, that ye be not judged. For with what judgment ye judge, ye shall be judged: and with what measure ye mete, it shall be measured to you again. And why beholdest thou the mote that is in thy brother's eye, but considerest not the beam that is in thine own eye? Or how wilt thou say to thy brother, Let me pull out the mote out of thine eye; and, behold, a beam is in thine own eye? Thou hypocrite, first cast out the beam out of thine own eye; and then shalt thou see clearly to cast out the mote out of thy brother's eye.

The rather terrifying aspect of Nostradamus' prophecy is what seems to have stung them. But St Thomas Aquinas, recounting a vision of St Catherine of Siena's, wrote: 'The Prophecies which come from Me [Christ] at first inspire terror, and are fulfilled in a sense of security.'

That I have been attacked by so many different people has in some respects reassured me, especially on rereading Luke 6:26: 'Woe unto you, when all men shall speak well of you! for so did their fathers to the false prophets.'

In the sixteenth century the words 'astronomer' and 'astrologer' meant roughly the same thing. They embraced the science of astronomy and of the planetary influences described by Ptolemy, who had carried on the work of his predecessor, Hipparchus. Today the terms have very different meanings, and the confusion between them generally infuriates only the astronomers.

Some contemporary astrologers are knowledgeable scientists, well aware of the laws of celestial mechanics. They are all too rare, however, and for the most part shun publicity. One or two of them have written me interesting letters, passing on valuable information. I am grateful to them.

Superficiality, amateurishness, vanity, jealousy, stupidity and inaccuracy are just some of the constant failings displayed by the unfortunately far more numerous and vocal group of fake astrologers who were roused to anger by my first book. They should have felt far more concerned by Nostradamus' own condemnation of themselves: 'Omnesque Astrologi, Blenni, Barbari procul sunto.' (Let all astrologers, fools and barbarians keep off.)

Instead, they lay claim to understanding Nostradamus better than anyone else through some fantastic 'system' or other! They call themselves experts in the Centuries, and consider that no one but themselves has the ability or the right to approach the subject. Which doubtless explains why they see in Nostradamus a means of making a living rather than any genuine intellectual interest. It also, of course, explains their hostility towards me, which will only increase upon reading this. Let them consider the following comments by Chrysale, from Molière's *Les Femmes Savantes:* 'Do not strive to find out what goes on upon the moon, but concern yourselves a little with your own affairs, where we see everything going topsy-turvy.'

'Few men can without some stirrings of envy pay homage to the success of a friend.'

Aeschylus (525–456 BC)

'A prophet is not without honour, save in his own country, and in his own house.'

Matthew 13:57

The publication of *Nostradamus: Countdown to Apocalypse* taught me that in France, at least, the achieving of bestseller status is far from restful. This is especially true if such fame is unforeseen, and one has been abruptly hauled out of provincial obscurity and deposited on to the front pages.

Success is usually frowned upon. Critics of every sort impute to authors a host of Machiavellian intrigues in order to explain away what is, mostly, simply the fruit of their own labours. I was welcomed in other countries, such as Britain, Belgium, Spain, Switzerland and Germany. None of the many readers of my book whom I met could understand the hostility I had encountered in France. Here I except the French Canadians, to whom I am grateful for their unfailing courtesy and open-mindedness.

The book has been translated into a dozen languages and translations are in progress in scores of others. It has created work, generated revenue and brought in foreign currency. I can thank my own country for such recognition . . . but I have also begun to understand why successful Frenchmen have gone off to more receptive, less hostile countries than their native land.

Within months of the success of my book, no fewer than ten other works on the same subject were published in France, several by firms which had originally rejected my own manuscript. These attempts to climb aboard the bestseller bandwagon ranged from insult to plagiarism, by way of imitation, piracy and the reissue of old editions, with new or carefully revamped covers. Here is a list, in order of appearance, of the bandwagon climbers.

France

The Prophecies of Nostradamus by Serge Hutin (Belfond,1972). Reprinted in 1981 with new cover and corrections, the latter the result of plundering my book.
Nostradamus Betrayed by Elisabeth Bellecour, Introduction by Albert Slosman (Laffont, 1981). Ninety-nine of its 284 pages are taken up with misrepresenting and indeed insulting my father and myself. The cover itself incorporates a prime lie. It boasts: 'Complete and original text of the ten Centuries, from the 1605 edition.' I myself have worked from this 1605 Lyon edition of Benoit Rigaud's: it comprises twelve Centuries, plus sixains, presages, the Letter to César and the Letter to Henri, Second King of France. Yet these two individuals called me an impostor!
The Real Centuries and Prophecies (Nice, 1981). Reprint of the 1611 Troyes edition of Pierre Chevillot. At least it is complete and decently printed.
The Prophecies of Nostradamus by J. Q. Laroche-Valmont (S.I.P.E., 1981). A piracy of my own book and duly withdrawn by law. This work appeared in September 1981 with a cover which boasted: 'The book which predicted Mitterrand's victory!' What was more, it also quoted some appreciative comments lifted from reviews of my own book.
A Guide to Nostradamus by Jean-Paul Clébert (Lattès, 1981). A very

incomplete dictionary of Nostradamus' vocabulary, compiled mainly from Le Pelletier, Colin de Larmor, Reynaud-Plense and the definitions established in my book. Nostradamus' text, as I have pointed out, is liberally misprinted in many of the old editions. The above author is blithely unaware of most of them, and, even more hilariously, cannot distinguish between the letters *s* and *f*, which in sixteenth-century typography were interchangeable. His compilation accordingly reads like a nonsensical riddle.

Nostradamus' Reply to Jean-Charles de Fontbrune by Jean Robin (Editions de la Maisnie, 1981). A lightweight concoction with many references to occultists and alchemists, such as Paracelsus and Nicholas Flamel. The author repeats the Slosman-Bellecour slanders (q.v.), in particular the curse levelled against me by those two 'authors'. Robin conveniently avoids mentioning what happened on 25 October 1981. On that date Albert Slosman, appearing on television, again threatened me with the so-called curse of Nostradamus which was, in fact, his own invention.

Before he could leave the studios, however, Slosman suffered a coronary; he died three days later – ironically, my birthday.

Nostradamus, Prophecies from Today until AD 2000 (Florian, 1982). An insipid 93-page mini-compilation, consisting of various interpretations drawn from commentators and incorporating further attacks against myself.

Darkness: The Prophecies. An anonymous booklet which repeats the mockeries of Slosman and Bellecour.

Nostradamus' Jam Recipes, selected and adapted by F. Guérin. (Orban, 1981).

Handbook of the Magical Formulae of Nostradamus and Other Contemporary Sages (S.E.I.T.E.C., 1981). Adapted and translated from the Italian.

The Testament of Nostradamus by Daniel Ruzo (Editions du Rocher, 1982). Reprint of a 1975 book. I can scarcely reproach my own publishers for getting on the bandwagon when rivals were doing so with such gusto.

Germany

Nostradamus, Weissagungen über den Atomkrieg by Rudolph Putzien (1981). Reprint of a 1958 book.

Nostradamus, prophetische Weltgeschichte by Alexander Centurio. Reprint of a 1977 book.

Die grossen Weissagungen über die Zukumft der Menschheit by A. Voldben. Reprint of 1975 edition.

Nostradamus, Prophezeiungen bis zum Jahr 2000 by Andrée Wollher (1981). A piracy, withdrawn by law.

Die grossen Prophezeiungen des Nostradamus in moderner Deutung by Kurt Allgeier (1982).

Italy

Centurie e Presagi by Renuccio Boscolo. Reprint of 1972 edition.
Nostradamus, le Profezie by Carlo Patrian. Reprint of 1978 edition.
Italian version of *Handbook of Magical Formulae* (see under French bibliography).

Belgium

1981–2000: Twenty Years Which Will Transform the World by P. L. B Emir (Bolen). A 115-page booklet, some of whose interpretations are fairly obviously derived from mine.

Numerous other books in a variety of languages including Japanese have appeared. The Nostradamus 'industry' has also resulted in an (unsuccessful) pop record in France, and in Chrysler of Quebec using a bust and a quatrain of Nostradamus in order to promote a new model of car. Indeed it should be emphasized that it is the aberrations of our consumer society which are to blame for the world recession!

THE THIRD WORLD WAR

One of the most frequent accusations levelled against me is that I have profited by 'doom-mongering'. Yet scarcely a day passes without my reading newspaper headlines like: 'Western Fears of War', 'Europe at the centre of WW3', 'War: the French Army's Role', 'Three Scenarios of Apocalypse', 'Will Europe Burn?' etc. So who does in fact indulge in doom-mongering?

Public opinion is being gradually prepared for the notion that a Third World War is inevitable, as though (and this is certainly true for the arms dealers and manufacturers) it were the only way to resolve the world recession and reduce increasing unemployment. Nostradamus certainly never promoted such views, nor do I. I have always held to the belief that the only solution is in total multilateral disarmament, conventional as well as nuclear weaponry included.

At the time of writing (June 1982) and since the first volume of my book appeared in France, the planetary situation seems to have taken a distinct turn for the worse. We have seen President Sadat's assassination; an attempt on the Pope's life (13 May 1981); the Iran-Iraq War; the military coup in Poland (13 December 1981); the Falklands War; and, most disturbing of all in the light of Nostradamus' prophecy, the new Palestinian-Israeli wars. During the latter conflicts, Beirut the city of Hashem (cf. Letter to Henri, Second King of France) has been besieged and attacked by numerous armies (Israeli, Lebanese, Palestinian, Syrian, Falangist Christians, etc.) and largely destroyed. All these dramatic events are like warning lights on the dashboard of history in motion.

What then have the United Nations done to intervene during this period? They have uttered pious platitudes termed 'resolutions', which have never yet resolved any important question. In wars the principle of 'might is right' has always obtained and the creation in the twentieth century of international organizations such as the UN has not altered it.

Every day war gains a little more ground from peace. The main reason for this is because the planet is over-armed. It is surely absurd for the industrialized countries, which have vested interests in producing weapons of destruction, to sell huge quantities of armaments to what are called 'developing' countries. The latter's economies, the most severely hit by the world recession, are unable to ensure such development; in fact most of them are markedly impoverished, underdeveloped – with all that that implies in terms of starvation and misery.

Mao Tse Tung once wrote: 'War can be abolished only by war. It is necessary to take up the rifle so as to ensure that rifles are no longer required.' This statement is as false and malicious as the Romans': 'If you want peace, prepare for war.' Perhaps if the majority of mankind stopped accepting war as an inherent factor in man's nature we could escape from the age-old vicious circle.

Such deeply entrenched attitudes do not leave us much room for hope that wars will end on this beleaguered planet. But we can turn to and take heed of the prophetic messages of Nostradamus and the biblical prophets (despite the numerous tribulations announced by them, especially for our present century, with its two world wars to date).

Nostradamus clearly predicts (in his Letter to Henri, Second King of France) a universal peace, that celebrated Golden Age which, according to an astrologer I met in Montreal, should start in March 2023. In the same text Nostradamus writes: 'And at this juncture such a great pestilence begins that more than two-thirds of mankind shall perish.' Man is thus warned against the follies he can continue to perpetrate. He saw that modern warfare with its appalling methods of destruction – whether nuclear, bacteriological, chemical or conventional – can lead to catastrophes imperilling the entire human race.

So I hope that political leaders and heads of state will at once try to prove Nostradamus and his translator wrong. Let the warmongers, arms dealers and manufacturers be outlawed. To end war, the means of waging it must be extirpated. For a start, all governments, through their intermediary (the so-called United Nations), should organize a worldwide referendum, which would surely have the approval of ordinary people everywhere, asking the simple question: 'Should there be world disarmament?'

The fact that murders of and assassination attempts against men of peace and goodwill continue is a clear sign of the impending Apocalypse prophesied in Revelations. Men like Gandhi, Martin Luther King, Sadat and Pope John Paul II are apostles of peace over and above their particular religious beliefs. In a climate of violence and war they herald the universal peace predicted by Nostradamus and this is why they are the targets of the warmongers.

During the last few years various books have been published which promise or forecast a Third World War. Some of these are truly alarmist and all the more credible since their authors are high-ranking officers and experts on warfare. Those so-called rationalists, who invariably deride or attack Nostradamus because they cannot explain away the phenomenon of prophecy, might well inveigh against these purportedly 'reasonable' books which actually scare the public infinitely more. I list here just a few of these works, in chronological order:

The Third World War by General Sir John Hackett (Collins, 1979).
1984: The Apocalypse? by Pierre Jean Moatti (Lefeuvre, 1980).
The Apocalypse Has Already Begun by Claude Duvernoy (Editions du Guetteur, Switzerland, 1980).
How We May Lose the Third World War by General Robert Close (Belfond, 1981).
Who's Afraid of the Eighties? by Nicholas Mélot (Le Rocher, 1981).
Before the War by Cornelius Castoriadis (Fayard, 1981).
War Tomorrow by Patrick Schmoll (C.L.E.P.S., 1981).
War Today? by Jacques Depret, Preface by General Close (Le Rocher, 1982).
1982–1984: Three Years To Disrupt The World by Pierre Jean Moatti (Schrotter, 1982).

My own first book also tried to warn man, but through the medium of prophecies, to curb his aggressive propensities. I must sadly acknowledge its ineffectiveness, to date, in this respect. Special mention must be made here of the US bestseller *Freeze* by Senator Edward Kennedy. One 1982 reviewer maintained that it was partly due to this book and to the subsequent pressure of American public opinion that President

Reagan did a virtual U-turn in policy and began talking arms reduction to the Russians. It is true that Kennedy's book effectively exploits fear and terror, but I do not begrudge him its success: his book proved effective on the political front, where mine, alas, did not!

'Every reader collaborates in every book.'
Maurice Barrès (1862–1923)

After the first volume of this book appeared I received thousands of letters from readers. Many asked me a wide variety of questions which I was quite unable to answer individually. I trust that they will accept my apologies and my thanks for their support. Out of thousands of letters, only three were abusive; each of these was anonymous. This second volume thus gives me an opportunity to reply generally to most of the questions the letters posed.

1. Where should one settle or move to in order to escape war?

This was one of the most frequent questions, and during the twentieth century scarcely anyone has been able to give a satisfactory answer. This century war has spread so cancerously that it has affected countries, regions and communities which had previously lived in tranquillity far from aggressive Europe, the initiator of both world wars. It is a terrible regression where mankind is concerned, and yet there were theologians who believed that Apocalypse had arrived with the Battle of Verdun in 1916. For centuries supposedly Christian Europe had crusades, wars, the Inquisition, religious strife and bloody revolutions of all kinds, and managed to export quite a few to other continents.

If the phenomenon of war has become both endemic and epidemic, where can one take refuge? Nowhere, of course. We have to put our faith in divine providence. The media widely reported the following cautionary anecdote: two Canadians, quite convinced of the imminence and inevitability of a Third World War which Canada could not escape, decided to emigrate to a place that would be safe because it was isolated, poor, virtually unpopulated and had an uninviting climate. They researched various possibilities before discovering their haven of peace far from all artillery and bombs. The couple then duly departed – to the Falklands.

Let us imagine that in 1940, in order to escape the bombs raining on the capital, a Londoner decided to take refuge in Commonwealth territory, somewhere far-flung and safe from the European theatre of conflict.

He might conceivably have chosen a promising tropical paradise in the Solomon Islands – Guadalcanal. That, of course, was the scene of the most bloody fighting between the Americans and Japanese between August 1942 and February 1943.

My answer, then, is not an evasion – I have merely concluded that our entire planet now lives in a state of insecurity.

2.   Queries on Nostradamus' letter to Henri II

Many readers have asked for an interpretation of the Letter to Henri, Second King of France, and this text, included for the first time (see pp. 59–80), is of prime importance. It reinforced much of what I had translated previously and also helped me to be more precise on certain points. Thus Babylon, as mentioned by Nostradamus in the Letter to Henri and in three quatrains (CVIII, Q96 and CX, Q86 in Vol. 1, and CI, Q55), was translated in Vol. 1 according to the dictionary definition as 'large centre, such as Paris or London', whereas Nostradamus was making parallels between the history of the three German Reichs and that of Babylonian persecution (under three kings) of the Jews. In both cases the persecution lasted approximately three years.

3.   Did Nostradamus prophesy through divine inspiration?

Throughout his book of prophecies Nostradamus, within the confines of his code, is specific and concise. This in itself constitutes one of the main problems as regards understanding his work. The only time Nostradamus departs from his particular conciseness is when mentioning the origins of his vision into and across four and a half centuries of history. Like a *leitmotiv* the divine source of his inspiration is stressed on numerous occasions, especially in the Letter to César (see Vol. 1). And in the very first quatrain of the first Century, Nostradamus states once again: 'a small flame comes out of the solitude and brings things to pass which should not be thought vain'. Here he is alluding to the Holy Spirit, symbolized by the tongues of flame descending on the Apostles' heads at Pentecost. We should remember that in the Middle Ages the descent of the Holy Spirit was re-enacted by symbolic actions, one of which was the dropping of lighted tow from the eaves and galleries of churches and houses.

The second quatrain of the first Century affirms: 'divine splendour, divinity itself, sits beside him' (in order to dictate its message). Those who insist that Nostradamus must have used occult means, or that he drew his prophecies solely from planetary configurations, are contradicting Nostradamus' numerous affirmations of his divine inspiration.

Nostradamus specifically said in the Letter to César that 'understanding created by the intelligence cannot be acquired in occult fashion'. The language of Nostradamus is therefore the language of faith.

In 1981, after a brutal military coup had flung many thousands of Polish workers in jail, there remained only their own indestructible faith with which to celebrate a Christmas, barely a fortnight later, of utter penury and hardship. There were pious noises of regret from the West, which carried on revelling and carousing, while the Poles were on their own – a people martyred yet again.

And while Beirut, the peaceful capital of the 'Switzerland of the Middle East', was turned into a hell, Westerners calmly watched World Cup soccer from their armchairs. The Lebanese have only their faith left, be it Moslem, Christian or any other. And it is not true to say that this is all Israel's doing, for the Russians and Americans have surely had a hand in the affair too.

The Iran-Iraq War, the Lebanese situation, the Falklands War, Afghanistan etc. all keep the munitions factories busy for as long as they continue. And the spectre of unemployment haunts us. . . .

4. Is there a scientific explanation of prophecy?

No, given the current state of scientific research and knowledge. Here I would like to suggest a possible line of research in order to try to understand the prophetic phenomenon.

Paul Langevin, who publicized Einstein's Theory of Relativity in France, formulated in 1913 a theory known as the 'paradox of the twins'. To summarize: a pair of twins, A and B, will diverge at a precise point in time and space (such and such a spot at such and such a second). Twin A describes a straight line, twin B a curve of space-time and their respective trajectories will intersect at a second point. Their travelling speeds remain less than the speed of light (300,000 km/sec).

Twin B, subjected to acceleration, has aged less rapidly in transit between the two points than twin A. It is as if the first twin has remained stationary on earth while the second has travelled in a spacecraft. In other words, twin B has regained in time the greater amount of space covered in relation to twin A.

This paradox, not really paradoxical at all, has been observed using particle accelerators: an unstable particle, when projected at a speed close to that of light, has a shorter life than when at rest.

In 1971 the Americans verified this paradox convincingly. They placed an atomic clock in a Boeing and another on the ground, both synchronized. An atomic clock is accurate to 10^{-14} second. The airborne clock, moving eastwards as a second airborne clock moved west, 'gained' 59±10 nanoseconds while the one moving westward lost 273±7 nanoseconds (10^{-9} second).

The paradox allows us to suggest the proposition of a spacecraft projected at the speed of light whose crew cover in a given period T (for terrestrial time) space equivalent to several light years. At the end of one cosmic 'year', twin B, the traveller in space, would find on his return to earth not just that his twin had died, but he would also probably be confronted with another civilization altogether.

As regards the prophetic phenomenon, let us imagine that Nostradamus is twin B and Henri II, the king during whose reign Nostradamus prophesied, is twin A. Nostradamus will 'travel' in a few days or months through 450 years of history, yet without this section of man's history being predetermined, since he would have been 'living' it before his own contemporaries and hence before twin A. This would explain his comments on man's free will in the Letter to César, his son, also the question of man's full responsibility for the catastrophes he had seen during his 'voyage'. Doesn't this extract from the Letter to César link Nostradamus with Einstein four hundred years later?:

Eschewing any fantastic imaginings, you may through good judgement have insight into the future if you keep to the specific names of places that accord with planetary configurations, and with inspiration places and aspects yield up hidden properties, namely that power in whose presence the three times (past, present, and future) are understood as Eternity whose unfolding contains them all. . . .

5. Was Nostradamus influenced by the Cabala?

I did try to trace any such influences in Nostradamus' writings, but found none.

I participated in a 1982 Nostradamus symposium during which Dr Isidore Simon, an authority on the history of the Jews in Provence, lectured interestingly on the Marranos (Jews compelled to convert to Christianity), who nonetheless continued secretly to observe various Judaic rituals and traditions. Dr Simon correctly stressed that Nostradamus was neither a Marrano nor even descended from one, because his great-great-grandfather willingly became a Catholic convert. It should be remembered that the Jewish community in a sixteenth-century town had its own quarter: contacts between Jews and Catholics were as rare as those between Catholics and Protestants. Under the historical circumstances, it is surely inappropriate for so many occultists and esoteric devotees to claim that Jewish 'initiates' could have conveyed their secrets to a devout Catholic – one, moreover, received at the French royal court.

6. Are extra-terrestrials mentioned in the Centuries?

Not unless particular quatrains are wilfully distorted. Thus some interpreters have chosen to identify the 'great and terrifying leader' who will
come 'from the heavens' [ciel = heaven or sky. Tr.] during the seventh
month of 1999 (cf. CX, Q72, Vol. 1). They forget that aviation has
progressed so rapidly during the last few decades that thousands of troops
can be transported tens of thousands of miles in a few hours. What
technical advances, then, might there be between now and the year 2000?
Designers already have on their drawing boards plans for planes capable
of transporting several thousand men per flight. Nostradamus, too, had
quite enough to concern him upon earth without his looking further
afield, to the moon or elsewhere.

7. What about Nostradamus and chronology?

Everybody would like to read the future, arranged in chronological order
as in the history books. In this, too, looking to Nostradamus' prophecies
would prove futile. He states himself in his Letter to Henri, Second
King of France that had he wished he could have dated each quatrain,
but that this would not have pleased one and all. For this reason his text
is comprised of mere scraps of time – temporal hints and dates are
codified.

   History, as taught in schools, unfortunately tends to turn into a dreary
succession of events juxtaposed willy-nilly, without proper explanation
of those causal links which would allow us to understand such events.
Besides the judgements he passes on statesmen or political regimes,
Nostradamus the historian establishes links of cause and effect between
different events, sometimes even when these are greatly separated in
time. Thus in one quatrain he connects French 'usurpation' (a value
judgement indeed) of the Maghreb (North-west Africa) by the Third
Republic with the fall of the Fourth Republic in 1958 (cf. CIII, Q59,
Vol. 1). How should such a quatrain be classed – under the history of
the Third or of the Fourth Republic? The interpreter has, then, to make
an arbitrary choice when (as here) both hypotheses can be equally well
sustained.

8. What use have you made of computers?

In 1981 I took part in a German television programme on Nostradamus.
When I saw the German interviewer at my home, he showed me various
articles from the French press in which my use of a computer was
discussed. He pointed out that critics had been dismissive of this idea.

On a previous occasion I had mentioned to him that none of these hostile critics had come to visit me and that I wondered how they could have written as they did without even bothering to see for themselves. Eventually I took him into my office and showed him my *two* computer files. He remained nonplussed and asked why I had not shown these to my detractors. I would happily have done so, had any of them wanted to see them!

I showed him an article in the specialist magazine *Telesoft*, written by Patrick Coston, with whom I had spent a couple of hours, and who had questioned me at length not only about my use of computers but also on the whole subject. Patrick Coston's opinion was as follows:

De Fontbrune is certainly no charlatan. He is a remarkably erudite historian and linguist, who knows Latin, Greek and the ancient sixteenth-century French Nostradamus used. If the logic of his procedure were not so rigorous his interpretations would certainly not be so impressively convincing. What is more, some curious coincidences have backed up his revelations. . . .

So, far from denying the whole phenomenon of prophecy as so many sceptics do, Coston kept an open mind – the constructive attitude which has enabled man to cure major diseases and to progress from discovering the wheel to landing on the moon.

As to programming and how I use my systems, that will remain my own secret for the time being. I have been criticized for not revealing the names of the programmers who have worked for me. They themselves wished to remain anonymous, but here in this second volume I thank them all for their invaluable assistance.

9. *What is the point of revealing numerous prophecies of disasters?*

What if the purpose of such prophecies of disaster were to avoid or alleviate certain catastrophes? Revelations, Matthew, Chapter 24, and the Books of Ezekiel, Jeremiah, Isaiah and Daniel are all, if anything, gloomier than Nostradamus. And what about the notorious Third Secret of Fatima, still jealously kept by the Roman Catholic Church itself? Would that message be worse than my interpretations of Nostradamus' prophecies?

The use of a prophecy predicting disasters for man is, once revealed, to lead each individual to reflect on the dangers inherent in the world in which he or she lives and also on the responsibility of those in power everywhere, especially those motivated by corruptive power alone. The second stage of the prophetic message is only evident if, unhappily, the predicted catastrophe actually occurs. The prophecy then becomes a source of comfort, a refuge for all those ordinary folk who have been sucked unwillingly into the whirlpool of conflicts over which they have virtually no control. Prophecy fulfilled is, finally, the only circumstantial evidence – or at least a strong defence case – for the existence of God, the Supreme Being. Throughout history, one of man's most enduring characteristics has been to acknowledge the existence of some force greater than himself. Cartesianism has been unable to explain away that particular phenomenon. One can but observe it. Curiously enough, civilizations decline when they abandon their gods – that is, the metaphysical or spiritual principle. This change in thinking leads to a materialism whereby men seek only to satisfy physical needs, needs almost always artificially created. And the decadent civilizations then brand as 'barbarians' those who fall upon them in order to seize their possessions.

10. Nostradamus and 'Grand Chiren' or 'Grand Henric'

The prediction concerning a future King of France was probably one of the main (if unadmitted) reasons for French hostility towards my book. On this one issue there was unanimous opposition to my interpretation from the entire bourgeois French intelligentsia, Left and Right alike. The reason is quite clear.

French politicians adhere more rigidly to a political system than to that liberty which their system should respect. When in Spain for the launch of Vol. 1's Spanish edition, I met numerous journalists who asked me about the Bourbon leader mentioned by Nostradamus. This prediction particularly interested them since a Bourbon descendant of Louis XIV is currently on the throne of Spain. In 1975, when Juan Carlos succeeded General Franco, the French media were indulging in gloomy forecasts of what might happen to this 'Fascist stooge'. The Spanish people were expected to rebel against him, expelling him as swiftly and dramatically as possible. Actually – and this bears out my comments on French political behaviour – the French were the prey of wishful thinking, for their predictions never came true.

In 1981 Lieutenant Colonel Tejero planned his abortive military coup against the Spanish Parliament: Juan Carlos I was seen to risk his own life by barring the rebel advance. The next day Carillo, leader of the Spanish Communist Party, while emphasizing that he was no monarchist, paid special homage to the King for saving democracy in Spain. This was a fine example of the democratic spirit.

As for the 'Grand Chiren', some critics have even disputed this anagram of Henric (abbreviation of the Latin Henricus). But Nostradamus had foreseen this very controversy, since he seems to have given his friend Jean-Aimé de Chavigny the key to the word. Chavigny, who came from Beaune in Burgundy, stayed several times with Nostradamus at the latter's house in Salon, Provence. In 1594 he produced a bilingual (French and Latin) book, printed on Pierre Roussin's press at Lyon, called *The French Janus*, which is the first attempt to interpret the Centuries. This is what he wrote about the word Chiren:

> It was the last age, a royal Dame,
> Carrying in one hand an imperial crown,
> In the other a globe upon which read
> (Great mystery) Chiren, forming when turned
> The sacred name Henric; set at the world's head
> He must one day command that round machine.

Certain commentators maintain that Nostradamus' own quatrains about this Chiren refer to Henri IV, but Jean-Aimé de Chavigny is specific: he maintains 'the last age' signifies the last period of Nostradamus' prophecy, the twentieth century.

Readers have asked me who this future king would be, and for details about his origins, astrological background, etc. Such questions are impossible to answer. On 17 June 1940 (to make just one comparison), no one could have guessed that as from the next day a certain Brigadier Charles de Gaulle would begin playing a major role in the history of France.

11. *Is the predicted comet Halley's?*

Many of my readers believed that the extraordinary comet described by Nostradamus (CII, Q41, Vol. 1) was Halley's. Nothing of the sort. It must be emphasized that many thousands of comets travel through the solar system. Astronomers discover on average two or three of them every year. Since these are invisible to the naked eye, there is little publicity and only scientists know about and study them. When with the aid of a telescope a comet is discovered, it takes three or four months from that moment to the perihelion, the comet's passage round the sun. Almost as much time elapses before it disappears from sight. Not having any light of its own, it borrows its light from the sun, as does the moon.

In 1973 the Czech astronomer Kohoutek discovered a comet which was named after him. Scientists indulged in calculations that proved false: these were the errors which led to its being dubbed 'the comet of the century', and therefore more significant than Halley's Comet. In the circumstances, few could see it without a telescope. One important and far-reaching event (for it precipitated the world economic crisis) did 'coincide' with Kohoutek's perihelion: the Yom Kippur War.

Bearing in mind the characteristics of comets, let us return to the one announced by Nostradamus. Several readers have pointed out to me that a comet which appears on 21 June and which is visible to the naked eye for seven days cannot possibly disappear on 13 December, since seven months rather than seven days separate these dates. To answer this objection I should point out that it *is* possible, since the comet can be discovered (hence known about) on 21 June, can enter the perihelion at the end of September and be visible to the naked eye for seven days, disappearing in December. Readers must accept my apologies for not supplying these explanations in Vol. 1.

So the predicted comet is therefore still unknown, and if Nostradamus is to be believed, it will be far more important than that of Halley. Indeed, if two 'suns' are to be seen in the sky (i.e. the comet will be visible by day), it will be very unusual and implies an exceedingly large comet.

12. It has been claimed that Nostradamus never in fact foretold the destruction of Paris. Is this a de Fontbrune prophecy?

First of all, I am neither a prophet nor a clairvoyant of any kind. Some critics have challenged my interpretations of CVI, Q4 (Vol. 1):

> Le Celtique fleuve changera de rivage,
> Plus ne tiendra la cité d'Aggrippine
> Tout transmué, hormis le vieil langage,
> Saturn. Leo, Mars, Cancer en rapine.

Interpretation

The banks of the French river [the Seine] will change their appearance. Paris will no longer last. All will be transformed except the French language, for it will be a time of totalitarianism, war and misery caused by looting.

My detractors claim that this actually refers to the American destruction of Cologne in 1945, since the ancient name of this town is Colonia Agrippina. I was well aware of this interpretation, borrowed (unattributed) from Serge Hutin by the critics.

Common sense refutes this hypothesis. Is Cologne, Agrippina's city, *really* situated on the banks of a French river on French (*Celtique*) territory? This typically 'Nostradamic' trap has fooled most people, because the Cologne theory is an attractive solution – but for the simple fact that the city is not on a French river. . . .That is why I opted for Paris: the Seine is the 'French river' *par excellence*, and as such waters the capital.

Nostradamus' phrase 'the great city' always refers to Paris. This expression recurs in Sixain 52 and CIV, Q8 (both dealing with the

Mons. le M.d Daubigné ayant donné à Fontbrune lieut. en second de la charge de lieutenant en la Comp.e de grenadiers de … camp dont mon reg.t de … que vous commandez, vacante par la mort de Cambe … je vous écris cette lettre pour vous dire que vous ayez a le recevoir et faire reconnoitre en lad. charge de tous ceux … ainsy qu'il appartiendra, et la présente n'estant pour autre fin, je prie Dieu qu'il vous ayt Mons. le M.d Daubigné en sa s.te garde, écrit au Camp de la Commanderie du Vieux Joue le sept Juillet 1747.

Louis

Le P…r de … d'argenson

Jean-Louis de Fontbrune's orders, dated 7 July 1747, and signed by Louis XV

Massacre of St Bartholomew's Eve, Paris, 1572), and again in CIII, Q50 (the Siege of Paris, 1870). In CV, Q30, as well as the 'great city' reference, Paris is actually named.

Unfortunately, however, there are even more unequivocal quatrains. I shall quote two of them, to make it quite obvious that I am not inventing this disastrous prophecy. First, CVI, Q43:

> Long temps sera sans estre habitée,
> Où Seine et Marne autour vient arrouser,
> De la Tamise et martiaux tentée,
> Deceus les gardes en cuidant repousser.

Interpretation

The confluence of the Seine and Marne will remain for a long time uninhabited when the warriors attacking England will think about driving back her defenders.

Since 1555 such an event has been unimaginable, which is why I have 'placed' it in the future (see Vol. 1).

CIII, Q93 is even clearer, and specifies that Avignon will become the French capital – another prophecy I have been accused of inventing:

> Dans Avignon tout le chef de l'Empire
> Fera arrest pour Paris désolé:
> Tricast tiendra l'Annibalique ire,
> Lyon par change sera mal consolé.

Interpretation

The capital will be moved to Avignon because Paris will be destroyed. The Tricastin will be the cause of Moslem anger. Lyon will be very upset by the change of capital.

The front page of *Le Monde* (10 January 1975) ran the following story: 'Financing the Tricastin nuclear plant: Iran lends a billion dollars to the French Atomic Energy Commission in return for a 10% share in Eurodif.' Thus the Tricastin complex was part financed by the late Shah. In 1555 who would have connected Tricastin, a rural district of the small Drôme department of France, with the Arab world? Who if not Nostradamus? *Le Figaro* (4 December 1979) began an article: 'Franco-Iranian Problems: Iran's holding in Eurodif, the uranium refinery of Tricastin, has been frozen by the Paris Chamber of Commerce. This measure involves repayments of almost a billion dollars agreed upon by Teheran in 1975. . . .'

13.   Why were you accused of scare-mongering?

A widely syndicated interview with Marie-Thérèse de Brosses (*Paris-Match*, 17 July 1981), engendered considerable publicity for my book both in France and abroad. In this lengthy interview one important passage was ignored by the media, almost without exception. A great many magazines dwelt only upon the disasters Nostradamus had predicted since 1555. Well, weren't the two world wars appalling disasters? And was Nostradamus wrong to warn the generations to come? Surely not, I maintain, for thanks to the prophecies man is more than ever responsible for his follies, since he commits them knowingly.

I reproduce here the relevant passage from the *Paris-Match* interview:

J.-C.de F.: 'The Greek word 'apocalypse' means revelation and *not* appalling catastrophe or destruction, as it has come to mean currently. This revelation will be vouchsafed to man after 1999.'
M.-T.de B.: 'What was Nostradamus' purpose in publishing the Centuries?'
J.-C.de F.: '*To bring man a message of hope.*'
M.-T.de B.: 'I fail to see the hope in all the calamities he predicts for us!'
J.-C.de F.: 'He proclaims that the Apocalypse is going to bring man an era of extraordinary prosperity: the Age of Aquarius, the Golden Age. The Golden Age will return, he says so in his Letter to César, but meanwhile mankind will undergo the direst tribulations. . . .'

Two world wars, Hiroshima and Nagasaki, the French wars in Indo-China, the Korean War, the Algerian War, the Vietnam War, Cambodia and, more recently, Afghanistan, El Salvador, Nicaragua, Ethiopia, Angola, Iraq and Iran, the Falklands, the Middle East, Lebanon – aren't all these wars and revolutions actual catastrophes far more frightening than a book of prophecies?

In a 1981 review of a Morris West novel the journalist Jacques Cabau wrote 'One of a horde of imitations in the wake of current interest in Nostradamus. Approaching the year 2000, Apocalypse is in the air, and Morris West is its prophet.' Cabau concludes: 'West is no Graham Greene, but he exploits men's great millennial fears and his novel ends by pulling out all the stops, on a note of suspenseful ambiguity where fiction gets dangerously close to an uncertain reality.' But West did not have to put up with the sort of insults and lies which I came in for.

A 1982 article in *Le Monde* contained an account of the death of Michel Fazilleau, who killed himself using a method described in *How to Commit Suicide*, a book by Claude Guillon and Yves Le Bonniec. The journalist commented: 'This is the first accredited case directly linking any death with this book's publication. Its publisher is not surprised. He was expecting something of the sort.'

My book is not known to have caused any suicides, and those who were scared by it were those who went to see films like *Jaws*, *Towering Inferno*, and *Earthquake*. Will disaster movies now be banned?

14. How do you arrive at the equation 3797=1999?

In his Letter to César, Nostradamus wrote: 'I have composed books of prophecies, each containing one hundred astronomical quatrains, which I wanted to condense somewhat obscurely. The work is comprised of prophecies from today to the year 3797. This may perturb some, when they see such a long time span. . . .'

Most commentators have taken the date 3797 quite literally. I was not content to do so because one must always bear in mind that Nostradamus 'condensed', deliberately obscured or codified his texts – by his own admission. Nostradamus dropped a sly, even humorous, hint when he stated that some people might be put off by such a distant date, i.e. 3797. Why should he have written that, had not this figure concealed some sort of trap for the interpreter?

But there is an even more obvious clue here. There was no need to give this 'date' and then add 'from today to', for it is surely self-evident that since his letter is dated 1 March 1555, and as he is talking of prophecy, his quatrains cannot refer to any earlier date. This tautology is untypical, for Nostradamus' style is concise.

The phrase 'from today to the year 3797' must therefore be looked at carefully, as though it were strictly mathematical: when in mathematics one says 'from point A to point B', it indicates a straight line, and Nostradamus is indicating between point 1555 and point 3797 a precise segment of time. The value of this segment of time is calculated by subtracting the former from the latter, and the result is 2,242 years.

This should be carried over to the biblical chronology given in the Letter to Henri, Second King of France, i.e. 4,757 years from Adam to Christ. If one adds to these 4,757 years 2,000 years AD, the result is 6,757 – which does not make up the full seven millennia. I believe this is the reason why Nostradamus 'fabricated' this extra segment of time – in order to cover the 242 years required to reach the year 7000 according to global chronology (6,999-6,757=242). By adding this segment of 2,242 years to the biblical reckoning one obtains 4,757 + 2,242=6,999 (i.e. 1999 AD, a date clearly specified in CX, Q72.

Two quatrains corroborate this calculation. The first, included in Vol. I, is CI, Q48:

> Vingt ans du règne de la Lune passés,
> Sept mille ans autre tiendra sa monarchie
> Quand le soleil prendra ses jours lassés,
> Lors accomplir et mine ma prophétie.

Interpretation

After twenty years of republican power, another will establish the monarchy until the seventh millennium [1999]. When this monarchy knows misfortune [Latin *lassae res:* ill fortune] then shall my prophecy be accomplished and terminated.

The second quatrain, CX, Q74, is from this second volume and concerns the first resurrection announced in Revelations 20:

> Au revole du grand nombre septième,
> Apparaîtra eu temps jeux d'Hécatombe:
> Non éloigné du grand âge millième,
> Que les entrés sortiront de leur tombe.

Interpretation

When the seventh millennium is reached, there will then take place a veritable hecatomb which will happen near the millennium. Then those who have entered the tomb will emerge from it.

All this confirms what I have always maintained – that Revelations, like Nostradamus' prophecies, is a message of hope. This knowledge may be a comfort during one of the darkest and most painful moments in the history of mankind.

As regards the end of the world, this does not concern us, our children or our grandchildren, since both Revelations and Nostradamus see this happening around 3000 AD, when the forces of destruction and misfortune are unleashed anew, following the thousand-year period of universal peace.

Abbreviations

AE	*ALPHA Encyclopédie*, 17 vols.
AVL	*Atlas Vidal-Lablache.*
AU	*Atlas Universalis.*
CUCD	*Chronologie Universelle*, Ch. Dreyss, Hachette, 1873.
DAFL	*Dictionnaire d'Ancien Français Larousse.*
DDP	*Dictionnaire des Papes*, Hans Kuhner, Buchet-Chastel, 1958.
DENF	*Dictionnaire étymologique des noms de famille*, Albert Dauzat, Librairie Larousse, 1951.
DGF	*Dictionnaire Grec-Français*, A. Chassang.
DH3	*Documents d'Histoire*, 3, Cours Chaulanges.
DH4	*Documents d'Histoire*, 4, Cours Chaulanges.
DHB	*Dictionnaire d'Histoire*, N. M. Bouillet, Hachette, 1880.
DHCD	*Dictionnaire d'Histoire*, Ch. Dezobry, 2 vols.

DL	*Dictionnaire Littré*, 4 vols.
DLLB	*Dictionnaire Latin*, Le Bègue.
DL7V	*Dictionnaire Larousse*, 7 vols.
DP	*Dictionnaire de la Provence et du Comté Venaissin*, Jean Mossy, Marseille, 1785.
DSGM	*Dictionnaire de la Seconde Guerre mondiale*, Jean Dumont, Historama, 1971.
DSH	*Dossiers secrets de l'Histoire*, A. Decaux, Librairie académique Perrin, 1966.
EU	*Encyclopaedia Universalis*, 20 vols.
GP & MR	*Garibaldi*, Paolo et Monika Romani, Les géants de l'Histoire, Fayolle, 1978.
HAB	*Hitler*, Alan Bullock, Marabout University, 1963.
HC4	*Histoire classe de 4*, Fernand Nathan.
HDA	*Histoire de l'Allemagne*, André Maurois, Hachette, 1965.
HDCAE	'Histoire de Chypre', Achille Emilianides, *Que sais-je?* no. 1009.
HDGM	'Histoire de la Grèce moderne', Nicolas Svoronos. *Que sais-je?* no. 578.
HDMJG	'Histoire de Malte', Jacques Grodechot, *Que sais-je?* no. 509.
HDVFT	'Histoire de Venise', Freddy Thiriet, *Que sais-je?* no. 522.
HEFDP	*Histoire d'Espagne*, Fernando Diaz Plaja, France-Loisirs.
HFA	*Histoire de France*, Anquetil, Paris. 1829.
HFACAD	*Histoire de France et des Français*, André Castelot et Alain Decaux, 13 vols, Plon et Librairie académique Perrin, 1972.
HFAM	*Histoire de France*, Albert Malet.
HFJB	*Histoire de France*, Jacques Bainville.
HFPG	*Histoire des Français*, Pierre Gaxotte.
HFVD	*Histoire de France*, Victor Duruy.
HRU	*Histoire du Royaume-Uni*, Coll. Armand Colin, 1967.
HISR	*Histoire de l'Italie, du Risorgimento à nos jours*, Sergio Romano, Coll. Point, Le Seuil, 1977.
HLFRA	*Histoire de la Libération de la France*, R. Aron, Fayard.
HSF	*Histoire de la Société Française*, L. Alphan et R. Doucet.
LCH3 et 4	*La Classe d'Histoire, 3, 4*.
LCI	*La campagne d'Italie*, Maréchal Juin, Ed. Guy Victor, 1962.
LDG	*La Dernière Guerre*, Ed. Alphée, Monaco.
LDR	*Le Dossier Romanov*, Anthony Summers, Tom Mangold, Albin Michel, 1980.
LFL XIV	*La France de Louis XIV*, Culture, Art, Loisirs.
LEGESGM	*Les Grandes Enigmes de la Seconde Guerre mondiale*, Ed. St-Clair, Paris.
LGR	*Les Guerres de Religion*, Pierre Miquel, Fayard, 1980.
LGT	*La Grande Terreur*, Robert Conquest, Stock, 1970.
LMC	*Le Monde Contemporain*, Hatier.
LMSH	*Le Mémorial de Saint-Hélène*, Las Cases.
LRFPG	*La Révolution française*, Pierre Gaxotte, Fayard.

LSEOA   *Le Second Empire*, Octave Aubry, Fayard.
LTR   *Le Temps des Révolutions*, Louis Girard.
LXIVJR   *Louis XIV*, Jacques Roujon, Ed. du Livre Moderne, 1943.
MAB   *Mussolini, le Fascisme*, A. Brissaud, Cercle Européen du Livre, Robert Langeac, 1976.
MCH   *Mussolini*, Christopher Hibbert, R. Laffont, 1963.
MGR   *Mythologie grècque et romaine*, Classiques Garnier.
NEE   *Napoléon et l'Empire*, Hachette, 1968.
NELGI   *Napoléon et la Garde Impériale*, Commandant Henry Lachouque, Ed. Bloud et Gay.
NLM   *Napoléon*, Louis Madelin, Hachette.
PCHF   *Précis chronologique d'Histoire de France*, G. Dujarric, Albin Michel, 1977.
PGB   *Pétain*, Georges Blond, Presses de la Cité, 1966.
VCAHU   *Vingt-cinq ans d'Histoire Universelle*, Michel Mourre, Ed. Universitaires, 1971.

2
THE EVIDENCE

What better way is there to reply to the sceptics than by pointing out the 'coincidences' between a number of events and various quatrains and sixains I translated up to and before May 1980 – when the manuscript of Vol. 1 went to press.

I am thus including in this chapter various texts from Vol. 1. To distinguish them from material newly translated for this volume, an asterisk precedes the title of all such texts. The cover of the 7 January 1982 issue of the magazine *L'Express*, bearing the headline '1981: SHOCK YEAR' provides perhaps both a good introduction and a good illustration. It features a long article looking back over the main events of 1981, with this introductory paragraph:

Another year ended – one which will leave its mark on twentieth-century history. Was the 1981 vintage good or bad? Let's not reply hypocritically: 'That depends.' It's almost impossible to list all the major events of the last twelve months – they're still happening. *For the French, it was the Year of the Rose, emblem of the new socialist government. . . .Abroad, coups, assassination attempts, wars. Poland, the Middle East, Iran, Afghanistan,* Africa, Indo-China, Latin America, Ireland, Spain: we live in ever more callous times, dominated by violence and threatened with a future none dare confront. *Pacificism itself could become dangerous.* . . . [My italics stress the particularly 'Nostradamic' comments.]

The article – to say the least – seems more catastrophic than pessimistic. No one was offended by it as they were by my book. Indeed, the article promises us sacrifices, violence and warfare. As regards the violence and warfare, *L'Express* was unfortunately all too accurate: riots in Paris, bloodshed in the Falklands, Iran, Afghanistan, the Lebanon. . . .

In 1980 no one had foreseen this shocking year – except for Nostradamus. I certainly did not – and I say this advisedly, after reading such a large number of articles that gave the impression that *I* rather than Nostradamus was the prophet! My sole aim was, and still is, to try to shed light upon what has been considered by too many people, for far too long, as meaningless nonsense.

MALTA AND LIBYA

* The Middle Eastern Origin of the Third World War

De l'Orient viendra le coeur Punique[1]
Fascher Hadrie et les hoirs[2] Romulides
Accompagné de la classe Libique,
Tremblez Mellites[3] et proches isles vuides.

CI,Q9

Interpretation

From the East will come the treacherous act which will strike the Adriatic Sea and the heirs of Romulus [Italians], with the Libyan fleet; tremble, inhabitants of Malta and its archipelago.

[1] *Foi punique:* bad faith. DL.
[2] Legal term for an heir. DL7V.
[3] Latin Melita: Malta DLLB.
See page 287 of *Nostradamus: Countdown to Apocalypse.*

History and commentary:

'*Malta: Base for Gaddafy?* At Malta a Libyan mission is turning the former British military airstrip at Hal Far into a helicopter base. There is concern in NATO circles that Col. Gaddafy, who maintains excellent relations with Maltese Prime Minister Dom Mintoff, is seeking to replace the British presence there, which ends on 31 March when the UK finally abandons her Maltese bases.' (*L'Express*, 20 January 1979)

This is exactly what did happen.

In its 9 February 1980 issue, *L'Express* wrote: '*Mediterranean Alert.* There are signs of covert Libyan involvement in Chad, the Sahara, Bangui and Gafsa . . .', while the ransacking of the French Embassy in Tripoli exposed Gaddafy's real schemes.

That leads me to the quatrains which directly followed the one above:

* Colonel Gaddafy Stirs up the Arab World against the West. The Great King: A Man of Culture against the Arabs

Prince libinique puissant en Occident,
François d'Arabe viendra tant enflammer
Scavant aux lettres sera condescendent,
La langue Arabe en François translater.

CIII,Q27

Interpretation

A Libyan chief of state, powerful in the West, will come to inflame so many Arabs against the French, then comes an educated and well-intentioned man who translates the Arab language into French.

See page 287 of *Nostradamus: Countdown to Apocalypse*.

History and commentary

Indeed, reporting the wrecking of the French Embassy at Tripoli, Christian d'Epenoux wrote: 'Since 28 January, the day after the attack on Gafsa by Libyan-trained commandos, Gaddafy's radio began a rabid hate campaign. Frustration is evident beneath all the triumphant communiqués and the interminable fantasizing speeches: this time *they had to rouse the Libyan masses against the French "aggressors" and direct their 'rightful anger' against them*. Matters came to a head on 4 February, when a crowd of 'spontaneous' demonstrators invaded the French Embassy, scaling the walls to ransack and burn the place. Vociferous young Libyans lowered the French flag and replaced it with the colours of the "Jamahirya". . . . That afternoon, *the same popular indignation was directed against the French consulate at Benghazi*, the country's second most important city, *and it too was destroyed. . . .*'

THE BOLOGNA STATION MASSACRE
2 AUGUST 1980

* The Revolution in Italy

Au lieu que HIERON[1] fait sa nef fabriquer,
Si grand déluge sera et si subite,
Qu'on n'aura lieu ne terres s'ataquer,
L'onde monter Fesulan[2] Olympique.

CVIII,QI6

Interpretation

In the place where God has built his Church [Rome] there will be so
great and sudden a revolution that no areas or lands will escape attack.
The revolution will reach Tuscany [Florence] after the Olympic Games.

  [1] Greek ἱερός: holy, sacred, divine. DGF. Allusion to Christ's words to Peter: ' . . .
on this rock', etc.
  [2] Faesula = Fiesole, town in Etruria (Tuscany). DLLB.
See pages 269–70 of *Nostradamus: Countdown to Apocalypse.*

History and commentary

This quatrain typifies the difficulties that face the translator of Nostradamus. I had translated *Fesulan* as Fiesole, whose Roman name was
Faesula. But Nostradamus had added an *n* on the end of the word, and
this could not be for reasons of paragoge, for such an addition was not
in order to aid the metre.

Bologna was in fact the town indicated, for its Latin name was Felsina
– from which Nostradamus makes an anagram here, substituting *u* for
i, which was then quite usual, these letters being typographically interchangeable at the time, as were *s* and *z*.

The Opening Ceremony of the 22nd Olympic Games, held in Moscow,
took place on 19 July 1980. On 2 August following, a powerful bomb
exploded inside Bologna railway station, killing 86 and injuring 200
more.

Rome had been the first major city affected by the revolutionary
movements in Italy, whether Left or Right. Aldo Moro's assassination
was the most spectacular exploit of the Red Brigades, which deeply
influenced public opinion in Rome.

Nostradamus makes it clear that few countries will escape terrorist
action of some sort: France, West Germany, Great Britain, Spain,

Ireland, Austria and Belgium are just some of the European countries involved. . . .

My error shows just how important it is to track down verbal minutiae in such a text.

AFGHAN RESISTANCE FIGHTERS BURIED SEPTEMBER 1980

* The Russian Invasion of Afghanistan. Afghan Resistance. Its Extermination

Le sainct empire[1] viendra en Germanie,
Ismaëlites trouveront lieux ouverts:
Anes[2] voudront aussie la Carmanie,
Les soustenans[3] de terre tous couverts.

CX,Q31

Interpretation

The Russians will come into Afghanistan; the Moslems will find these places open. The Afghans would like to keep Afghanistan; but the resistance will be buried.

[1] Russian Empire, the largest state in the world. Orthodox religion dominated Russia and the Tsar was its head since Peter the Great; the *Holy* Synod supported him in the administration of ecclesiastical affairs. DHB. 'Holy Russia' is a well-known expression.
[2] Certain Carmanian tribes, according to Strabo, led donkeys into battle. DL7V. Nostradamus refers to the Afghan resisters of the Soviet invasion.
[3] Latin *sustineo:* I resist. DLLB.
See page 328 of *Nostradamus: Countdown to Apocalypse.*

History and commentary

L'Express of 6 September 1980 ran an article on Afghanistan whose headline ran: '*The Buried Hospital:* Afghan Resistance Fighters Die Daily in Antiseptic Wilderness'. Patrick Laburthe's article described how two doctors from the International Medical Organization had helped construct an *underground* hospital from which wounded Afghan guerrillas unfortunately had only a slim chance of emerging, since it lacked even the most rudimentary antiseptics.

France-Soir reported a few days after this: 'Inhabitants of some Afghan villages relate that every evening after dark the noise of heavy bulldozers can be heard. Their sordid so-called *'excavation work'* is horrifying. Prisoners, teachers, intellectuals thought to be hostile to the regime, women and children too, were being *buried alive*, crushed and torn apart in the process.'

And Nostradamus in 1555 wrote 'the resisters will be covered by earth'. He also predicts that resistance to the invasion will continue.

THE ARMIES OF AFGHANISTAN AND IRAN. THE WAR BETWEEN IRAQ AND IRAN, 1981–82

* The Leader of Iran's Present to the West. The Attack on France and Italy Launched from Afghanistan

Le grand Satyre[1] et Tigre[2] d'Hircanie,[3]
Don présenté à ceux de l'Occean,
Un chef de classe istra[4] de Carmanie[5]
Qui prendra terre au Tyrren[6] Phocean.[7]

CIII,Q90

Interpretation

The great cynical person from the Tigris and Iran will make a gift to those of the Atlantic Alliance; then a military leader will leave from Afghanistan to land in the Tyrrhenian Sea and Marseille.

[1] Cynical or impudent person. DL7V.

[2] River in Asia, running into the Persian Gulf, in Iran.

[3] Hyrcania: region of ancient Asia extending along the south-east coast of the Caspian Sea, belonging to the Persian Empire. DHB. Today Iranian territory.

[4] *Istre*, form of *issir*: to go out, forth. DAFL.

[5] Province of the old Persian Empire, now part of Afghanistan. DL7V.

[6] Naples, important NATO base.

[7] Nostradamus adds *an* to the word *Phocée*, by paragoge and for the rhyme's sake. See pages 327–28 of *Nostradamus: Countdown to Apocalypse*.

History and commentary

In this quatrain Nostradamus mentions the Tigris and Iran. The main fighting in the war between Iraq and Iran has taken place, and continues, in and around the main towns of Bassorah and Abadan, both situated on the Tigris. It seems that Iraq may end up losing this war, and that a sort of northern front, involving Syria also, is under formation.

As for the Afghan army, *Le Soir* (28 April 1980) headlined: '5000 Russian tanks deployed along the *Afghan-Iranian* border' and the same article asked the question: 'Is so much armour and an undisclosed amount of missiles necessary just to "pacify" one country? *Doesn't this hide a far more important plan? What if this army moved into Iran tomorrow?*'

L'Express (21 May 1982) echoed *Le Soir*'s fears: 'Afghanistan: Soviet troops are now backed up by Mig 23 fighters and equipped with SA8 Gecko ground-to-air missiles capable of hitting their target at 6000 metres. American intelligence is said to be uneasy at the presence of this sophisticated weaponry, unnecessary for use against the Afghan resistance.'

Both papers, in articles two years apart, were asking Nostradamic questions without realizing it.

THE BALANCE OF POWER, THE USSR AND THE TYPHOON
9 FEBRUARY 1981

* The USSR and the War in Europe.
The USSR and Turkey

Des régions subjectes à la Balance[1]
Feront troubler les monts par grande guerre,
Captif tout sexe deu[2] et tout Bisance,
Qu'on criera à l'aube terre à terre.

CV,Q70

Interpretation

The regions subject to the USSR will come to trouble the mountains [the Alps] with a major war and will take prisoners of both sexes throughout Turkey, so that at dawn there will be cries from one country to another.

¹ Seventh sign of the Zodiac: the Egyptians consecrated Libra and Scorpio to the god of evil, Typhon (or Set) who, not content with this astronomical homage, also required the sacrifice of red-haired men. DL7V. There is thus a triple allusion to the seven Eastern Bloc countries; to the revolution (Typhon/Typhoon); and to the Reds.

² Contraction of *de le*. DAFL.

See pages 385–86 of *Nostradamus: Countdown to Apocalypse*.

History and commentary

Interpreters of this quatrain have all hitherto taken the word *Balance* to refer to the USA, because of the symbolic scales of justice.

I did not share this view for two reasons. First, I noticed that Nostradamus had written 'Balance' with a capital B, and the word was printed thus in all the old editions, even though it is a common noun. Secondly, it seemed odd to envisage the USA coming to initiate a full-scale war in the Alps, which Nostradamus simply called 'the mountains', referring to the most important mountain range in Europe.

So I came to the conclusion that the zodiacal sign Libra was intended, i.e. the USSR in symbolic terms. This mythological method of concealing the meaning through riddles is common in the Centuries.

The magazine *Le Point* (9 February 1981) ran an article on the USSR's new submarine, called the Typhoon, and I quote: 'The Typhoon is simply a nuclear submarine armed with nuclear missiles . . . but it is one and a half times larger than any of its Western counterparts. We can assume, then, that it is also capable of launching far more nuclear missiles with multiple warheads.'

As if this were not enough to confirm my interpretation, one reads elsewhere in the same issue: 'SALT: Row Over Typhoon. By coding information received from their new Typhoon missile, the Soviets are thwarting US surveillance attempts. It is proving impossible to confirm whether the new missile, still in the testing stage, has more than the fourteen nuclear warheads authorized by the SALT 2 agreement. The latter has not yet been ratified by the Americans, but its violation by the Russians could prompt the Reagan administration to follow suit.' It is not the USA but the USSR, then, which has named both a new type of submarine and a new missile Typhoon.

10 MAY 1981

* The Left in Power. Revolutionary Upheavals

Sur le milieu du grand monde[1] la rose,[2]
Pour nouveaux faicts sang public espandu:
A dire vray, on aura bouche close:[3]
Lors au besoing tard viendra l'attendu.

CV,Q96

Interpretation

When socialism is in power amid the bourgeoisie, the people's blood will flow because of new acts. To tell the truth, freedom of expression will disappear. Then the awaited helper will arrive late because of penury.

[1] *Grand monde:* expression for important, affluent, influential people as a whole or a class. DL7V.
[2] Emblem of Socialist party in France.
[3] To silence someone, i.e. make them keep their mouths shut. DL7V.
See page 278 of *Nostradamus: Countdown to Apocalypse.*

History and commentary

François Mitterrand was elected President of the Republic on 10 May 1981. The following month this victory was confirmed by a sweeping left-wing majority in the National Assembly. The first opinion polls in M. Mitterrand's favour appeared only a month before 10 May, six months after publication of the first volume of this book. The rose had indeed 'blossomed' in France (cf. the next quatrain). *Le Point* (27 April 1981) wrote: 'Mitterrand: Rosy Prospects. For the first time the Socialists top 25% according to opinion polls. On 22 May, the new President will be returned to office holding a rose.'

Nostradamus predicted in this quatrain that after the rose had arrived, civilian blood would be shed. One must not therefore expect assassination attempts against specific individuals, but blind terrorism directed against innocent passers by.

On 29 March 1982, less than a year after the change of government, a bomb exploded in Toulouse, killing 5 people and injuring 27 more. On 22 April 1982 a booby-trapped car exploded in Rue Marbeuf, Paris, leaving one dead and 63 injured. This incident prompted one French magazine to declare on its cover: 'Terrorism: War Declared on France'. On 21 July 1982 another bomb exploded – on the Place St-Michel, Paris

– wounding 11 people, 3 of them seriously. Since then the bloodshed has steadily increased and in the following months there were various incidents which 'made the people's blood flow'.

Le Point (16 August 1982) wrote: 'A year ago, in their prophecies about France, the most hardened pessimists might have put their money on an economic decline like England's or a breakdown of law and order like Italy's. Unfortunately their wager must remain open.'

* The Death of the Pope at Lyon. The Left in Power in France

> Romain Pontife garde de t'approcher
> De la cité que deux fleuves arrose:[1]
> Ton sang viendra auprès de là cracher,
> Toy et les tiens quand fleurira la Rose.[2]

CII,Q97

Interpretation

Roman Pope, do not approach the town which two rivers water [Lyon]. Your blood and that of your followers will flow near this spot, when the left gets into power.

[1] Lyon, whose two rivers are the Rhône and Saône.
[2] Emblem of the French Socialist party.
See page 277 of *Nostradamus: Countdown to Apocalypse*.

---

* Extract from *Prophecies of Maistre Michel Nostradamus, explained and annotated*, by Dr M. de Fontbrune (Cahors, 1958, 11th edition):

> Sur le milieu du grand monde la Rose[1]
> Par nouveaux faicts sang public espandu:
> A dire vray on aura bouche close
> Lors au besoing tard viendra l'attendu.

CV,Q96

Interpretation

Among people of importance, England, as the result of a new state of things, will see the blood of her people shed. . . .In fact, people will be forced to keep silent, but then, if required, the expected saviour will come in due course.

[1] Rose: symbol here for the Houses of York and Lancaster.

History and commentary

On 13 May 1981, three days after the election of Mitterrand, there was an assassination attempt against Pope John-Paul II, committed by a young Turkish Moslem fanatic in St Peter's Square, in the very heart of the Vatican.

These two quatrains (CII,Q97 and CV,Q96) were largely responsible for the publicity my book received, but the one about the Pope, in particular, was pressed into service by fantasizing interpreters who wanted to link Nostradamus' text to this specific incident at all costs. But the quatrain mentions a city on two rivers: the Vatican *City* itself stands on none. The misrepresentation experts then discovered two Roman rivers not in the Vatican City – the greater and lesser Tiber, which anyhow are only one river! I would advise all such fashionable disprovers of my reading of this quatrain that in Vol. I there are several more quatrains that make it clear that Lyon is being referred to, namely: CVII,Q22; CVIII,Q46; CVIII,Q62; and CIX,Q68.

As regards the word 'rose', I have been accused of misrepresenting Nostradamus' text by substituting a capital *R* for a lower-case one. There again my critics omit to mention that CV,Q96 in Vol. I is included with a lower case *r*, and that in both instances, capital letter or otherwise, I translated the word 'rose' as socialism! Had they wanted to research the matter properly, they would have seen that it is in my father's book that rose is written with a capital *R*. I merely forgot to correct one of the two. I would also add that I have found no edition, ancient or recent, giving the word 'rose' with a capital *R*. (I reproduce here verbatim the relevant passage from my father's 1958 book, in which 'Rose' is written with an initial capital and translated as England.)

Being familiar with this quatrain, I knew that the Pope's life would be in danger whenever (and not because) socialism gained power in France. The question that must be asked today is this: was the May 1981 assassination attempt a warning or a precursor of an eventual assassination – on 13 December at Lyon – of Pope John-Paul II?

An additional proof that this quatrain cannot apply to the 13 May

attempt is that Nostradamus wrote: '*toi et les tiens*' (you and your entourage) – and no member of the Papal escort was wounded.

Without wishing to draw any conclusion from them, I shall now list
various strange 'coincidences' that have struck me between the famous
prophecy of Fatima in Portugal and the attempt on John-Paul's life in
St Peter's Square on 13 May 1981.

The first 'vision' at Fatima occurred on 13 May 1917, announcing not
only the approaching end of the First World War, but also the installation
in Russia of an anticlerical and atheist power with all its attendant
executions and imprisonments.

The other appearances took place on the thirteenth day of the following
months until 13 October 1917, and the Bolshevik Revolution! On 13
May 1981, the shot which hit the Pope was fired at exactly 17.19, as
reported by numerous papers. Reversed, these paired numbers make 19
and 17, i.e. 1917. Over twenty-four hours, the number of combinations
possible between the minutes and hours is so great that the likelihood
of the assassination attempt occurring either at 19.17 or 17.19 is ex-
tremely slight.

In addition, the would-be assassin was a young Moslem fanatic. And
it is curious indeed that the town of Fatima, which bears the name of
Mohammed's daughter, was the site of these incidents.

Finally, in CIX,Q68, I 'interpreted' St Lucy's Day (and Lucia is the
name of the last survivor among the three children from Fatima) as being
13 December – the date of the *eventual* assassination of the Pope.

THE ASSASSINATION ATTEMPT AGAINST
JOHN-PAUL II AT FATIMA
12 MAY 1982

* The Traditionalists and Spain

Devant le lac où plus cher fut jetté
De sept mois et son ost[1] tout déconfit,
Seront Hispans par Albannois gastez
Par délay perte en donnant le conflit.

CVIII,Q94

Interpretation

Near Lake Geneva, where a more cherished [heresy: i.e. Calvinism] was launched, his supporters will be discomfited at the end of seven months. The Spaniards will be corrupted by the men of Albano [the traditionalists] and the conflict will be the reason for their loss.

[1] Crowd, troop. DAFL.
See page 299 of *Nostradamus: Countdown to Apocalypse*.

* The Schism and the Foreign Pope

Par chapeaux rouges querelles et nouveaux scismes
Quand on aura esleu le Sabinois[1]
On produira contre lui grands sophismes
Et sera Rome lésée par Albannois.

CV,Q46

Interpretation

Because of the cardinals there will be quarrels and a new schism, during which the Foreigner will have been elected. Great sophisms will be uttered against him and the Vatican will be harmed by the men from Albano.

[1] The Sabines were 'the foreigners' to the Romans.
See page 299 of *Nostradamus: Countdown to Apocalypse*.

History and commentary

On 12 May 1982, at Fatima, the Pope was the victim of an attack which the magazine *Spectacle du Monde* (no. 243, June 1982) described thus: 'Just as the Holy Father was leaving the Chapel a priest rushed towards him shouting "Down with the Pope!", "Death to the Council!" and "Death to Communism!" When arrested by the police, Father Juan Fernandez Krohn, *a Spaniard*, was found to be carrying a bayonet from a 1917 model Mauser rifle, as still used by the Portuguese Republican Guard. He confessed: "Yes, I wanted to kill the Pope." '

SOUTH AFRICA: A BASE FOR THE WEST? THE IMPORTANT ROLE OF SOUTH AFRICA IN THE THIRD WORLD WAR

* The USSR and the Warsaw Pact against South Africa. Fighting in Palestine

> Tost l'Éléphant[1] de toutes parts verra,
> Quand pourvoyeur au Griffon[2] se joindra,
> Sa ruine proche, et Mars qui toujours gronde:
> Fera grands faits auprès de terre saincte,
> Grands estendars[3] sur la terre et sur l'onde,
> Si[4] la nef a esté de deux frères enceinte.

> Sixain 56

Interpretation

South Africa will see [things happen] on all sides when the supplier [Russia] joins up with the Warsaw Pact. Her ruin approaches and the war which always rumbles will cause great upheavals near the Holy Land [Israel]. By land and sea there will be great military forces when the Church has given birth to two brothers [John-Paul I and John-Paul II].

[1] Olifant (from Latin *elephantus:* elephant). Name given to several mountains and rivers in southern Africa, after the elephants the first Europeans encountered there. The Olifant mountains are in the western part of Cape Colony, near a little river, the Olifant, which flows into the Atlantic. DL7V.

[2] Cf. CX,Q86 '*Comme un gryphon viendra le Roi d'Europe*'.

[3] Battle flag. DL7V.

[4] Latin: when, at such time as. DLLB.

See page 416 of *Nostradamus: Countdown to Apocalypse*.

History and commentary

After Ronald Reagan's election, Bernard Ullmann of *L'Express* wrote on 17 January 1981: 'The first spectacular initiative announced by Haig, and directly after the failure of the Geneva Conference on Namibia, is a tour of southern Africa which (excluding countries like Angola, under Cuban or Soviet control) will very probably take in South Africa. Such a visit would have been out of the question for a Democrat President.'

'Out of the question', perhaps, for politicians indulging in speculations and theories, but not for Nostradamus in 1555!

The sudden importance of South Africa in American eyes was confirmed by a report in *Le Monde* (12 June 1981), which began: 'South Africa: Visit by Haig's chief aide. Washington will now be pledging firm support for the Pretoria regime.'

PACIFISM – JULY 1981

* Pacifist Myths, Causes of Wars

Les Dieux feront aux humains apparences,
Ce qu'ils seront autheurs de grand conflict,
Avant ciel veu serein, espée et lance,
Que vers main[1] gauche sera plus grand afflict.

CI,Q91

Interpretation

Myths will mislead men because they will cause great wars, before which men will see the sky serene, then land weapons [*espée*] and aerial ones [*lance*] will be even more distressing towards the forces of the left.

[1] Latin *manus:* force. DLLB.
See page 264 of *Nostradamus: Countdown to Apocalypse.*

History and commentary

The Peace Movement's first great demonstrations began in July 1981, originating in West Germany and spreading throughout Western Europe.

L'Express (31 July 1981) wrote: 'The Pacifist Pandemic: Peace Movement gaining ground throughout Europe, with the exception of France.'

The same weekly (1 January 1982) wrote: 'Even pacifism could become dangerous', and 'What if pacifist theories led to a war of annihilation?' These questions were almost verbatim the same ones I had posed in analyzing CI,Q91 in Vol. 1, back in 1980. The language of *L'Express* was more explicitly 'apocalyptic' than mine, but the point is that in October 1980 the Peace Movement as such had not greatly flourished.

SADAT'S ASSASSINATION
6 OCTOBER 1981

* The Conference between Arabs and Jews

L'ire insensée du combat furieux
Fera à table par frères le fer luyre,
Les départir mort blessé curieux,
Le fier duelle viendra en France nuyre.

CII,Q34

Interpretation

The mad rage of furious battle will make swords shine even among
brothers seated at the same table; in order to decide between them, one
of them will have to be fatally injured in a curious way; their proud duel
will extend to harming France.

See page 289 of *Nostradamus: Countdown to Apocalypse.*

History and commentary

When identifying this quatrain with the Camp David Agreement, it was
impossible to tell which of the two signatories would be assassinated,
since Nostradamus had not been specific on that point. But in fact the
assassination of neither Sadat nor Begin (had the latter happened) would
have done anything other than destabilize the precarious balance of the
peace in that sensitive part of the world. The proof of this is the way
Egyptian policy towards Israel has changed since Sadat's assassination.
Definitely one of President Mubarak's most publicized actions was the
immediate release from prison of the Moslem Brothers jailed by his
predecessor.

On 6 October 1981 the road to Heliopolis ('the solar city' as Nostradamus calls it) was packed. Egyptians had turned out in vast numbers to
the festivities celebrating the anniversary of the crossing of the Suez
Canal by their troops eight years previously. The Raïs was on the stand
along with his Vice-President, Mubarak, various ministers and other
religious, political and diplomatic VIPs. It was one o'clock when an army
lorry from the procession halted in front of the grandstand. The driver
and six other men leaped from it and opened fire on the stand. The Raïs
fell, fatally *injured,* and died shortly afterwards. The media everywhere
stressed the extraordinary nature of this political murder, labelling it
'unprecedented' and *unusual.*

As for the 'proud duel', one can perhaps, without distorting facts, point to international terrorism spreading.

The first country to welcome the assassination of the 1978 Nobel Peace Prizewinner was Libya, followed almost immediately by Algeria. (See CIII,Q27 and CX,Q38, Vol. 1.)

We should remember, finally, that at Camp David Sadat and Begin had declared themselves to be blood *brothers*, in that one was a descendant of Isaac, the other of Ishmael.

MILITARY RULE IN POLAND
13 DECEMBER 1981

* Religious Persecution in Poland

Persécutée de Dieu sera l'Eglise,
Et les saincts temples seront expoliez,
L'enfant, la mère mettra nud en chemise,
Seront Arabes aux Polons ralliéz.

CV,Q73

Interpretation

The Catholic Church will be persecuted in Poland and the churches will be expropriated. The mother [Church] will be stripped naked by her children, and the Arabs will ally with the Poles [Warsaw Pact].

See pages 306–307 of *Nostradamus: Countdown to Apocalypse.*

History and commentary

Before 13 December 1981 my understanding and interpretation of the above quatrain were fiercely disputed by critics, who quoted it as an example of my so-called fantasizing.

Since the Catholic Church supported Solidarity, the persecution by the military authorities of Lech Walesa and the worker-members of his union was thus also a direct attack upon the Church. That alone would have upheld my interpretation, but there are further supporting facts. In April 1982 the magazine *Le Méridional* said: 'Poland: two priests face a military court. For the first time since the Stalin Era, two priests are to be charged – one with sedition, the other with receiving and concealing weapons. This puts the Polish Church, hitherto perhaps too influential, into a tricky situation within a country virtually under siege.'

As for the alliance between Arabs and Poles (to which I added as personal commentary 'Warsaw Pact'), the mass circulation Italian daily *Corriere della Sera* headlined an August 1981 article: ('Libya Warns: We Should Join the Warsaw Pact'). This in fact took place in September, aboard a Russian vessel of the Soviet Mediterranean Fleet in the Gulf of Sirte off the Libyan coast. An account in *L'Express* (5 February 1982) further verifies the interpretation of this particular quatrain: '*Poland: Exchanges With Tripoli*. More than 200 Libyan army cadets have just arrived in Warsaw to undergo special arms training. A member of the Polish military council recently met Gaddafy in Tripoli.'

As regards Poland persecuted 'by her own children', this was how *Le Méridional* (14 April 1982) reported a broadcast on Radio Solidarity: 'The female announcer criticized the authorities for "declaring war *on their own people*".'

THE FALKLANDS: WARNING SIGNS?

* From the Second to the Third World War. Great Naval Battles

> Un peu après non point long intervalle:
> Par terre et mer sera faict grand tumulte:
> Beaucoup plus grande sera pugne[1] navalle,
> Feux, animaux, qui plus feront d'insulte.

CII,Q40

Interpretation

After a not very long interval a great war will break out on land and sea. The naval combats will be the most important. The ferocity [of men] will be worse than the war itself.

[1] Latin *pugnum:* combat. DLLB.
See pages 264–65 of *Nostradamus: Countdown to Apocalypse.*

History and commentary

Philippe Bernert, in an article in *VSD* (17 June 1982), wrote: 'According to London, on this occasion informed by American intelligence, the Soviets would have used the Falklands War to good effect, by testing their methods of electronic surveillance . . . Admiral Woodward's adjutant explained to us that it was as if the Russians were intending to rehearse for a naval war they would one day wage. . . .

'In the end, Soviet assistance delayed the British victory by only one week. Yet it was also a victory for Moscow, this time a technological one. Soviet spy satellites can now observe any area of the globe.'

The correspondence between the quatrain and this journalist's 'vision' is striking.

THE FALKLANDS WAR
2 APRIL – 14 JUNE 1982

* Great Naval Battles in the Atlantic

Après combat et bataille navalle,
Le grand Neptune[1] à son plus haut befroy[2]
Rouge adversaire de peur deviendra pasle
Mettant le Grand Occean en effroy.

CIII,QI

Interpretation

After a naval combat, England will know her greatest alarm. Then the Soviet adversary will pale with fear, having sown terror in the Atlantic [or the Atlantic Alliance].

[1] God of the sea. Always symbolizes England.
[2] Belfry: tower with a bell for sounding the alarm. DL.
See page 347 of *Nostradamus: Countdown to Apocalypse*.

History and commentary

On 2 April the Argentine army invaded the Falkland Islands. Who could have foreseen, in 1980, that the UK would have been involved in a major sea battle in the Atlantic? Nostradamus did!

The media all noted that not since the Second World War had there been a naval battle on such a scale, during which a dozen ships, both Argentine and British, were sunk.

In my interpretation of this text, the Soviet Union was involved in the war, which was principally a naval conflict.

Philippe Bernert wrote: '. . . As a rule the Argentines were not in a position to pick up and decode such communications. They had no reconnaissance vessel or aircraft in the immediate vicinity of the Falklands. Yet they were informed in very great detail. Wave after wave of Skyhawks and Mirages carried out rocket attacks on the two large troop carriers, *Sir Tristram* and *Sir Galahad*. It was something of a massacre. . . .

' "The Americans refused to lend us their AWACS, which would have averted the loss of several ships," sighed one of Admiral Woodward's adjutants. "But the Russians *did not hesitate to pitch in against us*. . . ."

'From first indications, the Russians appear to have been apprised of Argentine intentions since March. . . .Indeed, the vast Soviet electronic surveillance system over the South Atlantic was operative well before the Argentine attack. . . .'

This journalist goes on to explain that the Russians had launched two spy satellites on 31 March, followed by a third on 2 April, the very day of the Argentine landings on the Falklands. As though this already sophisticated system were not enough, four other satellites, with varying yet precise objectives, were launched on 16, 21, 23 and 29 April.

'Black Tuesday' had caused England her *greatest alarm* since 1945.

EVENTS AT MARSEILLE, 1982

* Discord Among the French.
Internal Strife at Marseille

L'accord et pache sera du tout rompuë:
Les amitiés polluées par discorde,
L'haine envieillie, toute foy¹ corrompuë,
Et l'espérance, Marseille sans concorde.

CXII,Q59

Interpretation

The peace agreement will be completely broken. Alliances will be destroyed by discord. The old hatred will corrupt all confidence and hope. There will not be concord at Marseille.

[1] Latin *fides:* confidence. DLLB.
See page 270 of *Nostradamus: Countdown to Apocalypse.*

History and commentary

The Auriol and Lucet affairs, a judge's murder, the siege on 23 June of a Moroccan district of the town by taxidrivers, and, above all, a 'fake invoice' racket, directly implicating the council of France's second city, form proof enough of discord in the Phocean city.

The magazine *Le Point* (5 July 1982), carried the headline 'Marseille: The Big Swindle' and continued: 'Smell of Scandal at Marseille. Twenty-one people questioned, including eleven council employees. An unhappy affair.'

It concluded: 'Since the news broke, the authorities have suspended the council employees concerned. Gaston Defferre has stated he will take legal action. This course of action will not be sufficient to dispel *the poisonous atmosphere that has been created.* For this sort of racket could only have come about thanks to a whole network of complicity, nepotism and double-dealing which the police are gradually uncovering. *At Marseille, people are awaiting the next episode.* And the ones after that.'

THE FIFTH ARAB-ISRAELI WAR. THE FALL IN GOLD PRICES

* Peace Breaks Down in the Middle East. France and Portugal Hit by the Conflict

La foy Punique en Orient rompue,
Grand Iud,[1] et Rosne Loire, et Tag changeront
Quand du mulet[2] la faim sera repue,
Classe espargie, sang et corps nageront.

CII,Q60

Interpretation

Moslem duplicity will provoke a split in the Middle East. Because of a great person on the Jewish side, the Rhône, Loire and Tagus will see changes when the greed for gold has died down, the fleet will be engulfed, blood and sailors' bodies will be floating.

  [1] Latin *Judaei:* the Jews. DLLB.
  [2] Historical allusion: Philip, King of Macedon, used to say there was no impregnable fortress wherever a mule laden with gold could ascend. An expression of the irresistible power of gold. DL7V.
See page 291 of *Nostradamus: Countdown to Apocalypse.*

History and commentary

The magazine *VSD* (8 July 1982) reported that the Israelis had discovered a gigantic military complex being built underground in the vicinity of Sidon. This was going on while Yasser Arafat travelled on diplomatic public relations trips to Western capitals. It was undoubtedly the main reason for the Israeli invasion of Lebanon, since it enabled Israel to demolish not only the Sidon installations but also the Russian SAM missile bases on the Bekaa plain. This operation was initiated by a Jewish head of state, Begin, just when gold prices had been falling for several months (when hunger for the proverbial mule will be satisfied!)
  As regards the engulfed fleet, this probably refers to the dozen or so Argentine and British ships sunk during the Falklands War in the South Atlantic. Nine hundred Argentine sailors swam or floated until rescued, apart from 350 more who drowned.
  The possible sequence of events implied by this quatrain is hardly reassuring.

3
LETTER TO HENRI, SECOND KING OF FRANCE
Original text, interpretation and notes

This letter, with that to César reproduced in *Nostradamus: Countdown to Apocalypse*, page xx, is the second prose text of Michel de Notredame's prophetic work. In all the old editions (prior to 1610) it is placed between the seventh and eighth Centuries. In most of the post-1610 editions the letter has been printed at the start of the work, immediately after the Letter to César. This reorganizing of the texts might seem unimportant if the texts themselves did not vary. However, when I began working on the Centuries, twenty years ago, I followed the hypothesis that the position in the text of the Letter to Henri, Second King of France should provide the translator with a clue: namely, that it could not be properly 'decoded' until just over half the quatrains had been translated. That is why this letter does not appear in Vol. 1 of *Nostradamus: Countdown to Apocalypse*.

My own comments and interpolations are printed in italic; Nostradamus' own words are in roman type.

To the invincible, all-powerful and most Christian Henri, Fortunate King of France,[1] Michel Nostradamus his very humble and obedient servant and subject wishes victory and happiness. *[Most editions subsequent to those of Chevillot, Troyes, 1611[2] displace the word 'second' in this dedication address, so that 'Henry, Roi de France second' becomes 'Henry Second [or Henri II], King of France'].*

Because of the royal attention you have granted me, O truly Christian

---

[1] *Second*, from Latin *secundus*: fortunate, favoured, happy, auspicious. D.LAT. The adjective agrees with *Henry*, not *France*, and in this context the specialized Latinate usage rather than the more normal numerical connotation is always to be understood. [*Tr.*]

[2] Cf. Bibliography.

and victorious king, my face having been so long obscured,[1] I here
present myself before the deity of your boundless Majesty, and since I
was continually dazzled thereby, do not cease[2] to honour and justly to
revere that day when I presented myself before it for the first time, as
one does before such an extraordinary[3] and humane Majesty. Now, in
searching for an occasion to manifest to you my warm regard and frank-
ness with determination I would strive to make fuller knowledge available
for your most serene Majesty. To this end, it was not possible for me
personally to make these things known to you, despite my particular
desire to bring to your acquaintance the sudden illuminations which have
brought me from the darkness and shadows before the face of your
sovereign power[4] and of the first Monarch of the Universe. So long was
I in doubt as to whom I should dedicate these three final Centuries of
my prophecies which make up the thousand [quatrains], and I decided,
after long and due deliberation upon my rash audacity, to address them
to your Majesty, as one not astonished (as that gravest of authors Plut-
arch, in his life of Lycurgus, relates) by the sight of offerings and gifts
made as sacrifices within the temples of the immortal Gods of that age,
lest any be astonished that no gold or currency dare be presented.
Nonetheless, seeing that your Royal splendour is also linked to an incom-
parable kindness, I address myself to you not as one did to those Kings
of Persia with whom one could not seek audience, still less approach,
but as to a very sage and prudent Prince. Thus I have dedicated my
nocturnal and prophetic prognostications, composed thanks to a natural
instinct, with the aid of poetic transports, according to the rules of
poetry, and for the most part in accordance with the calculations of
Astronomy corresponding to the years, months and weeks, and to the
regions, countries and most of the towns and cities of all Europe,
including Africa and part of Asia that shall know frontier changes, and
which draw near in all these climes – the whole being composed as by
a natural technique. Those who would do better to mind their own
business will retort that while the rhythm is easy enough, to understand
the ideas is difficult. And yet, O most humane of Kings, the greater part
of the quatrains are so improper that one would not know how to make
sense of them, still less interpret them. I was hoping, however, to leave
behind in written form events which will pertain to years, towns, cities
and regions, even for the years 1585 to 1606, starting from today, 14
March 1557. And going well beyond these dates until the coming of the

---

[1] Latin *obnubilare* = *assombrir* = obscure. D.LAT.
[2] Latin *desistere* = *cesser* = cease. D.LAT.
[3] Latin *singularius:* rare or extraordinary. D.LAT.
[4] Latin *oculus:* eye or power. D.LAT.

beginning of the seventh millennium, through careful consideration, as far as my astronomical computation and other knowledge has allowed me to range: the epoch [*start of the seventh millennium*] in which the adversaries of Jesus Christ and His Church shall begin to multiply; the whole has thus been composed and calculated by selected and well-arranged hours and days, as correctly as possible. And I have made my prognostications concerning events in times to come with a free spirit and out of reach; using the past and understanding the present, for thus shall one know the future by the course of time through all regions; and as I here specify I have put in nothing superfluous, so much so that it may be said: rigorous exactitude about the future is not entirely determined. It is indeed true, Sire, that thanks to my natural instinct passed on to me by my ancestors[1] I could only believe I would be prophesying; I have therefore admitted and joined this natural gift to my lengthy calculation, while emptying my mind, heart and soul of all care, concern and worry in order to ensure calm and tranquillity of spirit. All was achieved and presaged and this in part thanks to the tripod.[2] As many people attribute to me what credit is mine as what is not; only eternal God, who alone truly knows the pious or brave works of men, is the judge, whose defence I solicit against the calumny of the wicked who would furthermore inquire to know how your own ancestors, Kings of France, cured scrofula or those of other nations healed the bites of serpents, or yet others had divinatory powers, and many other cases it would take too long here to recount. And so despite the malignity of the spirit of evil which will manifest itself in the course of time, after my death my writing will be better known than during my lifetime; and even were I to be mistaken in my calculation of epochs, none could do anything about that. May it please your more than Imperial Majesty to pardon me, protesting before God and His Saints, since I affirm that I have written nothing in the present letter contrary to the true Catholic faith, conveying the astronomical calculations in accordance with my knowledge: for the spaces of time, since the first men who preceded us, are such, and I start from the correctness of the most reputable judgement, that Adam, the first man, preceded Noah by 1,242 years, not calculating the times by Gentile reckoning as Varro has described them, but going solely by the Holy Scriptures and by my own weak intellect aided by my astronomical computations. After Noah, his day, and the universal flood, came

---

[1] Latin *avitus:* concerning one's ancestors. D.LAT.

[2] Greek Τρίπους: aloft, from a tripod, like the Sibyl. DG. Sibyls were the legendary priestesses of Apollo, endowed with the gift of prophecy. Erythrea was the most revered of these, as acknowledged by the author of the *Dies Irae* ('*Teste David cum Sibylla*'). David announced the end of the world, or day of wrath, as did the Sibyl. DL7V.

Abraham 1,080 years later, who was a remarkable Astrologer by all accounts, inventing the Chaldean alphabet. After him came Moses, 515 or 516 years later, and from Moses to David's time 570 years elapsed. Thereafter, from David to the time of Our Saviour and Redeemer Jesus Christ, born of the unique Virgin, 1,350 years passed: some might object that this reckoning is not accurate since it differs from that of Eusebius. And since the era of man's Redemption up to the detestable seduction of the Saracens, 621 years went by; from which one can readily calculate years past, although my reckoning is not good and valid for all nations because the whole has been calculated by the heavenly courses, along with intuitions in some subsecive hours and by the spirit of my distant ancestors: but the injustice[1] of our epoch, O Most Serene King, requires that these most secret events be manifest only by enigmatic phrases having but one sense and one meaning alone, without any ambiguity therein or doubtful calculation; but rather I profoundly obscured all by natural intuition, drawing closer to the language of the one thousand and two prophets acknowledged since the Creation of the world, according to the reckoning and to the Phoenician[2] Chronicle of Joel.[3] 'I will pour out my spirit upon all flesh; and your sons and your daughters shall prophesy'.[4] But such a prophecy proceeded from the mouth of the Holy Spirit, which was the sovereign eternal power, so that certain of these prophets, with the aid of the celestial movements, predicted great and marvellous happenings. But I do not here ascribe such a title for myself. Certainly[5] if it please God, I confess that all comes from Him and therein I render Him thanks, honour and immortal praise, without my having used divinatory methods derived from[6] fate, but thanks to God and my natural intuition, the whole in accord with the movement of heavenly bodies, so that I saw as in a burning mirror, as if by an obscured vision, the great, sad and prodigious incidents and calamities which affect most inhabitants.[7] First, God's Churches, secondly those purely material forces, will enter into such a decadence, with thousands of further calamitous events, and in due course of time the future will be known.

★ ★ ★

[1] Latin *injuria:* injustice. D.LAT.

[2] The Carthaginians, or Punic peoples (*Poeni*) were of Phoenician origin. DCEM. The Phoenicians were Semitic.

[3] Old Testament prophet, whose prediction of the Last Judgement in the Valley of Jehosaphat ends his book. Part of the Jewish canon, his book has always been regarded by the Church as inspired. DL7V.

[4] Joel 2:28 (AV). *Tr.*

[5] *Ia:* certainly, indeed. DAFL.

[6] Latin *provenire:* to grow, develop, derive from. D.LAT.

[7] Latin *cultor:* inhabitant or dweller. Virgil. D.LAT.

Nostradamus' general account of his prophecy ends here. Besides describing the divine origin of his nocturnal visions; his work methods and arrangement of the quatrains; the way he used 'coincidences' between planetary positions – by astronomy, and his chronology of man's history, this first section also gives a significant pointer both to the purpose and to the geographical boundaries of his vision.

This is of prime importance to the interpreter who, seeking to decode a great number of geographical names, should therefore look for cities, mountain ranges, rivers, villages etc. within the areas specifically mentioned.

To confuse the unperceptive, Nostradamus wrote that his quatrains are so 'improper [*i.e. unpolished*] that one would not know how to make sense of them, still less interpret them'. *Further on he stresses that his enigmatic phrases have one meaning and one only, and ends this first section with* 'the future will be known'. *This bears out a phrase in his Letter to César:* 'these things will be universally understood upon earth'. *The occultists and esoteric commentators who try (drawing on CI,QI, which refers to the bronze tripod) to prove that Nostradamus used divinatory methods (i.e. astrology, geomancy, necromancy, chiromancy etc.) cannot have read this important passage:* 'without my having used divinatory methods derived from fate, but thanks to God and my natural intuition'. *This statement carries additional weight, for it contradicts those who advocate that man's history is predestined – an unacceptable attitude which relieves man of responsibility for his acts and thus for his history. God would thus become a sort of sadist, amusing Himself by playing out a huge cosmic war game with men's lives. One can understand why Nostradamus, writing to César, therefore talks of man's free will.*

This is also why Nostradamus warns modern astrologers bound by Ptolemaic theories. Such inflexibility allows man only the despair of a life over which he would have neither responsibility nor control.

The conclusion (and this is borne out by the Old and New Testaments), is that prophecy is a warning to man. This explains why prophecies are generally of disasters, since their aim is to inform man of the misfortunes towards which he is heading through acts for which he is entirely responsible. St Thomas Aquinas, relating one of St Catherine of Siena's visions, wrote: 'The prophecies which come from Me [God] strike terror at first, but are fulfilled in a sensation of security.'[1]

At this point the prophetic section of the Letter to Henri begins. Nostradamus is to move back and forth through time, giving the impression (as in the

[1] *Introduction to the Theology of St. Thomas Aquinas*, R. Sineux (Paris, 1975).

quatrains), that he has set down sentences and phrases without any particular or precise order.

For God will watch the long sterility of the Great Lady, who shortly afterwards shall conceive two principal children. . . .

The phrase 'Great Lady', as used by Nostradamus, refers to the Queen (cf. Sixain 55, Vol. 1) whose descendants will not reign, hence the word 'sterility' as applied here to denote the end of the elder line of the Bourbons. Marie Antoinette, married in 1770, did not give birth to her first child until 1778. This was Marie-Thérèse Charlotte, Duchess of Angoulême. Her second child, Louis-Joseph, was born three years later, in 1781, dying in 1789. The third and last child, Louis XVII, was born on 27 March 1785. After Louis-Joseph's death, then, Marie Antoinette was left with two principal (surviving) children who would be imprisoned with her.

But [*the Queen*] being in peril, she will find herself in the fray[1] because of the audacity of the era of death [*the Terror*] endangering [*the monarchy*] in the eighteenth century, and it will not go beyond the thirty-sixth [*king*] and there shall remain three men and one woman.

Here Nostradamus places the end of the monarchy as the end of the eighteenth century, later giving the precise date, 1792. The main Bourbon line is to die out with the demise of Charles X, brother of Louis XVI. From Hugues Capet to Charles X there are thirty-six kings of France. The Capets comprise Hugues Capet, Robert II, Henri I, Philip I, Louis VI, Louis VII, Philip II, Louis VIII, Louis IX, Philip III, Philip IV, Louis X, John I, Philip V, Charles IV – a total of fifteen kings in the direct Capet line. Then come the Valois rulers: Philip VI, John II, Charles V, Charles VI, Charles VII, Louis XI, Charles VIII – a total of seven kings, followed by one Valois-Orléans, Louis XII, and the Valois-Angoulême line: François I, Henri II, Francis II, Charles IX and Henri III (five kings). These are succeeded by the elder branch of the Bourbons: Henry IV, Louis XIII, Louis XIV, Louis XV, Louis XVI, Louis XVII (six kings) and finally by Louis XVI's two brothers, Louis XVIII and Charles X.

After the disappearance of Louis XVII, there will thus remain three men who become king: Louis XVIII, Charles X and Louis-Philippe I, and one woman, Madame Royale, Marie-Antoinette's daughter.

Then there will be two emperors: [*Napoleon I and Napoleon III*] who will not have had the same father, besides the three brothers [*Louis XVI, Louis XVIII and Charles X*], who will be very different, then finally united and in accord, and three-quarters of Europe shall tremble.

Louis XVIII was at first with the opposition, whether in the Assembly of

---

[1] *Ajostée:* mêlée, engagement. DAFL.

Notables or in the States General, but after the first excesses, he declared himself for the counter-revolution.

The future Charles X, who entered Paris in April 1814, managed to conciliate most people with his friendly demeanour, but the goodwill towards him was soon dissipated when he signed, with a haste which even cast a slur on Louis XVIII himself, a treaty depriving France of her conquests since 1792.[1]

By going as far as Moscow, Napoleon I had indeed made three-quarters of Europe tremble. But allusion is also made here to wars waged by Napoleon III: the Crimea, Italy and the Franco-Prussian War.

During a shorter period [*in comparison with the thirteen centuries of continuous monarchical rule from 496 to 1792*], the Christian monarchy will be upheld and increased, the parties [*those of the French Revolution, i.e. Jacobins, Montagnards, Girondists etc.*] having suddenly risen to power but being just as quickly abased.

The Arabs will decline [*the conquest of Algeria began in 1830*], after Kingdoms have been created [*Napoleon I's creation of Kingdoms in Europe for his brothers*] and new laws having been promulgated [*the Civil Code*].

With other children [*Napoleon Bonaparte's brothers*], the first [*Napoleon I*] will occupy kingdoms comprising a Lion, which will be enraged because held in check by his relatives [*brothers*] thanks to the intrepidity of his armies.

The following kingdoms included a lion in their coats-of-arms or on their flags, and were occupied by Napoleon: Spain, Italy with the Lion of Venice, Belgium and the Netherlands. The same is true of a great many German provinces – Baden-Württemberg, Berlin, Rhineland, Bavaria, Hesse and Schleswig-Holstein.

The successor [*Napoleon III*] will invade so far into Italy that for the second time [*after Napoleon I*] the fury of war shall strike Rome.[2] He shall fall because of Spain. [*The candidature to the throne of Spain of Prince Hohenzollern, cousin of the King of Prussia, was contested by the French government. This opposition precipitated the Franco-Prussian War, the defeat at Sedan, and the fall of the Emperor.*] He will not be replaced by the ancient monarchy [*but by the Third Republic*]. And thus will come about the third inundation of human blood [*after the fall of the Ancien Régime. The first blood-letting was the Napoleonic Wars, the second the Franco-Prussian War and the third the 1914–18 War*].

And for a long time war will not be idle [*reference is made here to the wars of the twentieth century*].

[1] DHB.
[2] Jovis – for Jupiter. On the Palatine Hill in Rome are the Temples of Jupiter Stator and Victor, with another temple of Jupiter on the Capitol.

And the Republic[1] will be installed, which will cause the dominator [*the Tsar*] to fall with the help of a new pagan party [*Russian Communist Party*]. She will spawn two clans, one which will be faithful to her [Communist Party], the other which will remain unfaithful because of the encouragement of the Catholic Church.

Nostradamus refers here to the struggle which would develop after 1917 between the Communist party and the Catholic Church, especially in the Baltic States.

Then will be born another party [*Nazi*] which would like to ruin the former [*Communist*]; then there will be three regions which will create very different alliances, namely Italy, Germany and Spain, which will breed different parties by means of military coups.[2]

Nostradamus is predicting the creation of military dictatorships in Italy, Germany and Spain in their correct chronological order. Mussolini seized power in 1922 through his 'blackmail march' on Rome. In 1933 Hindenberg called Hitler to the Chancellery, and in 1936 General Franco came to prominence in Spain.

Leaving aside the fiftieth and fifty-second parallels. [*The fiftieth parallel crosses Cornwall, the fifty-second South Wales. Situated between the two, on the fifty-first parallel and thirty minutes, is London. Great Britain was to escape invasion during World War II.*]

And these countries will pay homage to the ancient religions[3] in the regions of Northern Europe [*Germany*]; beginning with the one on the fortieth parallel, which will tremble because of a useless fear; then shall tremble the most westerly, the most southerly and the most easterly. Their power will be such that they will form alliances and invincible unions through their warlike conquests.

The Nazi sects (the SS, SA etc.) would adopt the symbols and emblems of the Roman Empire, along with banners and huge, impressive military parades. This is why Nostradamus compares Hitler to Nero.[4] Madrid is situated on the fortieth parallel. The Spanish Civil War began in 1936, a prelude to the world war which followed. Then Hitler hurled his divisions westwards against Belgium and France. The Axis powers moved south, landing in Libya on 1 February 1941, and finally, on 22 June 1941, the Wehrmacht attacked the Soviet Union from the Baltic to the Black Sea. Moreover, in December 1941 the United States and Japan were at war also.

---

[1] Nostradamus frequently uses *fille* or *dame* to signify the French Republic (popularly symbolized as Marianne).

[2] Latin *manus:* force. D.LAT.

[3] Cf. CIII,Q76, Vol. I.

[4] Cf. CIX,Q17; CIX,Q53;CIX,Q76; and CVI,Q67, all Vol. I.

Here again Nostradamus lists the main theatres of World War II in their correct chronological order. The alliances formed by Nazi Germany constitute the historical term 'Axis powers'.

These military powers will be equal [*military regimes*] but very different in beliefs. [*Indeed there were considerable differences between Hitler, Mussolini and Franco, especially as regards their Asiatic ally, Japan.*]

Then a democracy still more powerful than the second [*France of 1789, after England*] will be received by two peoples [*USSR and China*], whose origin will be in the first democracy that has had power over all the world [*England and her power in the nineteenth century*] and then also in the second [*France*] and the third [*USSR*] extending its forces beyond Eastern Europe [*Asia*] as far as Hungary[1] which will have been conquered and occupied.

Nostradamus notes that the Soviet empire will extend both east and west after the fall of the Western European military dictatorships.

Then thanks to its navy the USSR will disembark[2] in Sicily[3] and the Adriatic after going through Greece[4] and [*West*] Germany, which will have succumbed, and the Arab forces after passing through Italy will be pursued and afflicted. Then the great empire of the Antichrist will begin in the Altai[5] Mountains and at Sevrej[6] whence he shall descend with innumerable troops, so that the coming of the Holy Spirit that advances along 48° longitude shall change place, pursued by the abomination of the Antichrist waging war against the great king [*Henri V*] who will be the great Vicar of Jesus Christ at the right and proper time; this event will precede the obscurest and darkest eclipse of the sun seen since the creation of the world, from the passion and death of Jesus Christ until then; then in the month of October there will be a great translatory movement, so much so that it will be thought the earth has lost its natural motion and is plunged into perpetual darkness. Before this there shall have been signs of the spring equinox[7] [*20 March 1999*].

In this passage Nostradamus puns upon Attila (whose epithet was The

---

[1] Pannonia: ancient Roman name for Hungary. DHB.

[2] Latin *exponere:* to disembark. D.LAT.

[3] Trinacria: name given to Sicily, because of the three capes in which the island ends. DHB.

[4] Myrmidons: name of ancient tribe in Thessaly (Greece). DL.

[5] Attila (Atila in French; *Tr.*) is an anagram of Altai: large mountain range in Central Asia, forming the northern edge of the great central plateau of Asia. It is divided into the Lower Altai, 47°55′ north by 80°155′ west, and the Higher Altai, south of Lower Altai, and north of Mongolia, on 48° latitude north. DHB.

[6] Zerfes: anagram of Sevrej, small town in the Lower Altai. AU. Note the equivalence of the interchangeable *f* and *v*.

[7] *'Point vernal'* – synonym for spring equinox. DL.

Scourge of God) and the Altai Mountains, to signify that, like Attila, the Antichrist will be born in Mongolia. As for the town of Sevrej, which Nostradamus writes 'Zerfes', it seems to have been transcribed phonetically, as if the name but not the spelling of the place had been dictated to him.

Nostradamus tells us that the Holy Spirit will be chased from the forty-eighth parallel. Not only does Paris lie on this, but also Ulan Bator, capital of Mongolia.

As in CII,Q72, Nostradamus precisely indicates that this invasion from Asia is to be launched before the eclipse of 11 August 1999, which will be visible in the Northern Hemisphere, along 48° longitude, and which will be total. He states that this invasion is to start in July 1999. In October of that same year there will be a natural phenomenon on a vast, global scale.

So as to be even more specific about this year, 1999, Nostradamus gives a point of reference (20 March) which allows us to situate the invasion threat.

And this will succeed extreme changes of power and revolutions,[1] with tremblings of the earth [*allusion to the tanks which are going to appear in the World War II theatres of operations*], with multitudes of the new Babylon,[2] unhappy daughter whose abomination will be increased by the first holocaust; and she will last only seventy-three years and seven months.

Nostradamus establishes a parallel between Nebuchadnezzar, who persecuted the Jews and led them captive into Babylon (now Iraq), and Nazi Germany's persecution of the Jews – to which history has now given that very same epithet 'The Holocaust'! As regards the duration of this new Babylon, German unity was born with the Treaty of Frankfurt, 10 May 1871, one of whose most important conditions was the annexation of Alsace-Lorraine.[3]

Between 4 and 12 December 1944, Alsace and the Saar were progressively liberated. From 10 May 1871 to 10 December 1944 there are precisely seventy-three years and seven months.

Then [*a branch*] will spring from the trunk that has long remained barren, and will come from the fifth rank[4] to renew the whole Christian church. And a great peace, union and agreement will be made between people[5] separated and lost because of the various powers. And there will be such a peace that the one who has originated and set in motion the

[1] Latin *permutatio:* revolution. D.LAT.

[2] Babylon: The Jews were held in captivity in this town for seventy years (605–536 BC). DHB.

[3] Cf. CVI,Q87, Vol. 1.

[4] Of nobility. Each generation counted since the first member of the particular family in question was ennobled. DL7V.

[5] *Front:* brow; in poetic terms, the actual person. DL.

warring faction against the diverse religions [*the Soviet atheistic and anti-religious system*] shall be cast into the depths of a prison[1] and the Country of the Violent[2] [*USSR*] shall be united, having played the sage.

Countries, towns, cities, powers and regions which will have abandoned the first paths they took [*Marxism*] in order to free themselves, shall be deprived of their liberty [*Hungary, Czechoslovakia, Angola, Afghanistan, Poland*], sinking into a deep captivity, and religion will be completely persecuted. They will begin by attacking the left [*Communist Party revisionists*] only to attack the right in turn, ruining[3] godliness for a long time with their own holy writ [*or Bible*]. After this great dog will appear the even greater hound [*the Antichrist*] who shall destroy all, even what had been destroyed[4] before him, after the churches are restored to their first state and the clergy functioning once again, then he shall spread debauchery and lust[5] and shall commit a thousand crimes.

This will come to pass shortly after another desolation [*World War II*], which will culminate in the military powers [*the Axis*] losing in two wars[6] [*the two world wars*] and they shall keep only[7] their flags [*allusion to the partition of Germany*].

These military powers will drag their nations into a swing towards the right [*fascist regimes*], when they will not want to accept putting out the cutting hand [*reference to the fascist salute*] and will affect the entire world [*world war*] until the birth of an offspring from that branch for so long sterile [*the Bourbons*].

This suggests that the Bourbon child will be born in 1945 or 1946, which would make his age today about thirty-eight.

He shall deliver the people of the world from this well-meaning[8] and voluntary servitude [*the countries opting for Marxist regimes*], being himself under the protection of Mars [*war*] which will have despoiled God[9] [*religion*] of honour and dignity, in order to liberate the town built and situated in another very small Mesopotamia [*Lyon, between the Saône and the Rhône*].[10]

---

[1] Latin *barathrum:* deep pit, after a ravine west of Athens, into which criminals were thrown, whose sides were planted with knives to cut the malefactors in their fall. DL7V.

[2] Latin *rabiosus:* fierce, violent. D.LAT.

[3] Latin *profligare:* to annihilate, ruin. D.LAT.

[4] Latin *perpetrare:* to achieve, execute, carry out thoroughly. D.LAT.

[5] Latin *mertricius:* trade of courtesan, prostitution. D.LAT.

[6] Sword – symbol of war and battle. DL7V.

[7] *Oter:* to take away, deprive of. DL7V.

[8] Latin *benignus:* generous, benevolent. D.LAT.

[9] Jupiter: father of heaven, ruling principle or God.

[10] Cf. CIII,Q46; CII,Q35; CIX,Q68; and CVIII,Q62, all Vol. I.

The head of the government [*Pflimlin in 1958*] will be expelled from power and swept away like a feather, unaware of the conspirators' plot: they will have at their head the second Thrasibulus [*General de Gaulle*], who for a long time will have organized all this affair.

Parallels drawn between the first Thrasibulus, the Athenian general during the Peloponnesian War (431 BC) and the second, General de Gaulle, are referred to in Vol. 1.

Then enormities and abominations shall shamefully come to the fore [*debauchery of the consumer society which will come into being after World War II*] and be manifest in the shadows darkening the spirit, and that will happen[1] towards the end of the change in his power [*allusion to May 1968, followed by the departure of General de Gaulle in 1969*]; and the heads of the Church will show themselves remiss when it comes to the love of God [*disputes in the Church*][2] and some among them will abandon the true faith, and of the three factions [*left, centre and right*] that of the middle [*or centre*] will be somewhat in decline.[3] The first [*the left*] shall win all Europe [*West Germany, France, Greece, Portugal, Spain etc.*] and most of Africa through the destruction of the third [*the right*], with the aid of the poor in spirit, who, thanks to demented people, shall establish corruption and debauchery. The people will rise up to resist[4] and attack those who would promulgate new laws; also it seems that the countries weakened by the Orientals [*USSR, Poland, Romania, Czechoslovakia, Hungary, East Germany and Bulgaria*] may be victims of Satan freed by the creator of infernal prisons, in order to bring to birth great Gog and Magog[5] who shall wreak so much abominable destruction upon the Churches that the reds [*Communists*] and the whites [*Moslems*] shall thereby lose their judgement, power and strength. And their power shall be taken from them. And then there shall be more persecutions of the Churches than ever before. And at this juncture such a great pestilence[6] shall begin that more than two-thirds of mankind shall perish. So much so that one will no longer know the owners of the fields and houses, and the grass shall grow above knee height in the streets of the towns. And the clergy shall endure a total desolation and the warmakers [*USSR*]

[1] Latin *cedere:* to walk, go, come. D.LAT.

[2] On 29 July 1968 Pope Paul VI published the encyclical *Humanae Vitae*, on birth control. It pronounced against the findings of the commission of experts convened by the Pope himself in 1963, and led to much debate and controversy within the Church. VCAHU.

[3] The elections of 23–30 June 1968 saw the Gaullists triumph. They ended up with 358 out of 458 seats in the Assembly.

[4] Latin *sustinere:* to resist. D.LAT.

[5] Many editions have 'Gog and Magoh' for 'Dog and Doham'.

[6] Germ warfare?

shall use[1] the events at Cairo[2] in order to go from Malta as far as the Var coastline[3] and the great straits of the Bosphorus[4] shall be opened [*by the Russian fleet*].

Then there will take place a landing on the beaches to deliver Spain[5] from the Moslem occupation. And none of these attacks will be negligible and the place where Abraham lived [*Sichem*][6] will be attacked by the venerators of the West[7] [*to liberate it*]. And the city of Hashem[8] [*Beirut*] shall be surrounded and attacked in great strength from all sides by armies. But their [*Soviet*] fleet will be weakened by the Westerners, and this country [*USSR*] will know a great desolation; her greatest cities shall be depopulated and those who enter therein shall serve the vengeance of the wrath of God.

This section from the Letter to Henri should be compared with Ezekiel 38:

Son of man, set thy face against Gog, the land of Magog, the chief prince of Meshech [*Moscow*] and Tubal [*Tobolsk*] and prophesy against him. . . . And I will turn thee back, and put hooks into thy jaws, and I will bring thee forth, and all thine army, horses and horsemen, all of them clothed with all sorts of armour [*tank divisions*]. . . . Persia [*Iran*], Ethiopia, and Libya with them; all of them with shield and helmet [*Russian armaments*] . . . Gomer [*Turkey*], and all his bands; the house of Togarmah . . . and many people with thee . . . in the latter years [*before 1999*] thou shalt come into the land that is brought back from the sword, and is gathered out of many people [*the State of Israel in 1948*], against the mountains of Israel, which have been always waste . . .[9] And thou shalt say, I will go up to the land of unwalled villages [*the kibbutz*]; I will go to them that are at rest. . . . So that the fishes of the sea, and the fowls of the heaven, and the beasts of the field, and all creeping things that creep upon the earth, and all the men that are upon the face of

[1] Latin *usurpare:* to make use of, lay claim to. D.LAT.

[2] Greek 'Ηλιούπολις: Heliopolis, i.e. City of the Sun, a town in Lower Egypt, was situated 11 km north-east of Cairo. DHB. Cf. cv,Q81, Vol. 1. Reference to President Sadat's assassination?

[3] Staechades: the four islands known by this name lie off the coast of the Var department of France. DHB. Cf. cvii,Q37, Vol. 1.

[4] Bosphorus, from a Greek word signifying passage or cattle track. DHB.

[5] Cf. ci,Q31; ci,Q93; and cviii,Q48.

[6] Abraham left Haran with all his family, and, aged seventy-five, came to live in Sichem. DHB. Today Tell Balatah, town in Transjordan, occupied territory since 1967.

[7] Jovialis: pertaining to Jove/Jupiter. D.LAT. The planet Jupiter was regarded as fortunate by astrologers. DL7V. Nostradamus thus denotes the West, its allies and its good fortune. Cf. Presage 32; Presage 129; and cx,Q73, all Vol. 1.

[8] Hashem, tenth incarnation of Albar, supreme god of the Druze. DL7V. The Druze live on and around Mt Lebanon. Nostradamus thus indicates Lebanon here.

[9] Cf. cii,Q19, Vol. 1.

the earth, shall shake at my presence, and the mountains shall be thrown down, and the steep places shall fall, and every wall shall fall to the ground.

Chapter 39 continues:

Therefore, thou son of man, prophesy against Gog, and say, Thus saith the Lord God; Behold, I am against thee, O Gog, the chief prince of Meshech [*Moscow*] and Tubal [*Tobolsk*]. And I will turn thee back, and leave but the sixth part of thee [*the six Soviet satellite states*], and will cause thee to come up from the north parts [*Russia*], and will bring thee upon the mountains of Israel. . . . Thou shalt fall upon the mountains of Israel, thou and all thy bands, and the people that is with thee. . . . And I will send a fire on Magog. . . . And they that dwell in the cities of Israel shall go forth, and shall set on fire and burn the weapons, both the shields and the bucklers, the bows and the arrows, and the handstaves, and the spears [*missiles*] and they shall burn them with fire seven years . . . [*disarmament?*]

There is a remarkable parallel between Nostradamus and these two chapters of Ezekiel, the vision of the former being centred upon France and Europe and that of the latter upon Israel and the Middle East. Ezekiel's vision is even darker than Nostradamus'. Nostradamus goes on:

And the Holy Sepulchre[1] shall long remain venerated, at evening,[2] under the universal contemplation of the sky, the sun and the moon; then the Holy Places [*Jerusalem*] shall be exchanged [*annexation by Israel*] and shall shelter a small herd [*numerically: the Israelis*] and a large [*in terms of its importance to the West*] and they will be adapted to profane ideas [*Christian and Moslem alongside Jew*].

O what calamitous affliction shall the pregnant women then know, and the main Oriental chief [*China*] will be moved by the USSR[3] which will have conquered the West, put to death and imprisoned its children and women; and thus shall be accomplished the prophecy of the royal prophet:[4] please heaven that the cries of the prisoners[5] be heard and that their sons be delivered from massacre.[6]

[1] The gospels recount how Joseph of Arimathea buried Jesus' body in a new tomb hollowed from rock and situated in a garden near the site of the crucifixion. In AD 70 the suburbs of Jerusalem were destroyed during the Roman army's building of fortifications. In the fourth century St Helena, the Emperor Constantine's mother, had the ground dug up, exposing the sepulchre. Eusebius relates how a vast construction site appeared on Calvary. . . . The Holy Sepulchre became a place of pilgrimage for Christians. DL7V. From the fourth century until 1999 – '*longtemps*'.

[2] *Serain*: evening, nightfall. DAFL.

[3] Septentrion: the north, used, along with the word 'Aquilon', to denote the USSR, 'The Empire of the North'.

[4] David, second King of the Israelites. Poet and prophet, he left the Psalms as his enduring literary bequest. DL7V.

[5] Latin *compeditus:* one whose feet are shackled. D.LAT.

[6] Latin *interemptus:* killed; *interemptio:* murder. D.LAT.

The Psalms of David constitute a promise of deliverance to the people of Israel. To quote some particularly interesting and relevant passages: Psalm 22: 6–7:

> But I am a worm, and no man; a reproach of men, and despised of all the people. All they that see me laugh me to scorn; they shoot out the lip, they shake the head. . . . [*verse 12*] Many bulls have compassed me: strong bulls of Bashan[1] have beset me round.

After this reference to antisemitism, the royal prophet speaks of the danger the Golan represents for Israel: this explains the outright annexation effected in 1981.
Psalm 46:

> God is our refuge and strength, a very present help in trouble. Therefore will we not fear, though the earth be removed, and though the mountains be carried into the midst of the sea. . . . There is a river, the streams whereof shall make glad the city of God [*Jerusalem*], the holy place of the tabernacles of the most High. God is in the midst of her; she shall not be moved. . . .The heathen raged, the kingdoms were moved: he uttered his voice, the earth melted. . . . Come, behold the works of the Lord, what desolations he hath made in the earth. He maketh wars to cease unto the end of the earth.

This passage guarantees that Jerusalem will endure, untouched by war. Like Nostradamus, David announces an important depopulation of the earth and the coming of a universal peace.
Psalm 83:

> For, lo, thine enemies make a tumult: and they that hate thee have lifted up the head. . . . They have said, Come, and let us cut them off from being a nation: that the name of Israel may be no more in remembrance. For they have consulted together with one consent: they are confederate [*the Arab League*] against thee. The tabernacles of Edom [*Jordan*], and the Ishmaelites [*Saudi Arabia*]; of Moab [*Jordan*], and the Hagarenes [*Saudi Arabia*]; Gebal [*tribes of Arabia Felix*], and Ammon [*Jordan*], and Amalek [*Egyptians of Sinai*]; the Philistines [*Palestinians from Gaza*], with the inhabitants of Tyre [*Palestinians from Lebanon*]; Assur [*Iraq*] also is joined with them: they have holpen the children of Lot [*head of the Moabites and Ammonites*]. Do unto them as unto the Midianites[2]. . . . Who said, Let us take to ourselves the houses of God in possession [*claims on Jerusalem*].

Nostradamus continues:
What great oppression will be wrought then upon heads of government and states, even those of Japan [*maritime and Oriental*], and their languages will be mixed in a great society [*UNO*], the Latin and Arab tongues,

---

[1] Today the Golan Heights.
[2] The Midianites, an Arab race who lived south of the Moabites, were defeated by Gideon. DHB.

through Carthaginian [*Libyan*] communication,[1] and all the heads of state of Asia shall be hunted, persecuted or exterminated, not by means of USSR forces, but in the century which is to come [*the twentieth, the aim of the prophecy*] because of three countries which have made a secret alliance and which lament[2] death and set traps for each other,[3] and this triumvirate[4] will renew itself for seventy years[5] and the renown of this party shall extend throughout the planet, and in spite of it, the sacrifice of the Sacred and Immaculate Host shall be carried on [*Poland, Lithuania etc.*] and two heads of the Soviet Union shall be victors over the Orientals [*Japan*] and there will be made among them such a noise and warlike tumult that all the Orient [*China*] will tremble with fright because of their brothers [*Japanese*], no brothers to the USSR. This is why, Sire, in this discourse, I include these predictions almost confusedly, and in order to know when each event will happen by counting the time which follows – is not necessary knowledge, or at least little in accordance with heaven. These predictions made with the aid of astronomy and other methods, and even by the Holy Scriptures, cannot not happen. Had I wished I could have put a calculation of time into each quatrain; but that would not have pleased everyone, and my interpretations still less, unless your Majesty granted me enough protection to do this, so as not to give slanderers pretext for attacking me.

Here Nostradamus takes up a theme he had already sounded in his Letter to his son César, repeating that his prophetic message will not be to most people's liking. (Indeed, criticisms of Nostradamus: Countdown to Apocalypse, *illustrate his point admirably!*)

However, I calculated that the years from the creation of the world to the birth of Noah came to 1,506 years, and from Noah's birth until the Ark was finished, that is up to the time of the flood, 600 years passed (it had better be established if the years were solar or lunar, or whether they took account of the mixture of ten [*days*][6] [*Gregorian calendar*]; Holy Scripture indicates that they were solar. And at the end of these 600 years, Noah entered the Ark and was saved from the flood. This universal deluge then lasted one year and two months. From the end of the flood to Abraham's birth there were 295 years. From Abraham's birth to

---

[1] Cf. CIII,Q27; CI,Q9; CV,Q14; and CIII,Q60 – pages 287, 288 and 289 respectively in Vol. I.

[2] Latin *queri calamitatem*: to lament one's misfortune. Caesar. D.LAT.

[3] Latin *insidiari*: to set traps or ambushes. D.LAT.

[4] Reference to the Troika of the Soviet system?

[5] Nostradamus has 'cut down' this time span in order to keep the 7 of 1917 and that of 70 – the length of time Communism will have to spread over the world, i.e. until 1987.

[6] In 1582 Pope Gregory XIII, aided by a Calabrian expert called Lilio, deleted ten days from the calendar to bring the equinox to 21 March.

Isaac's birth 100 years elapsed. From Isaac to Jacob, sixty years passed. From Jacob's entry into Egypt until his departure was 130 years. And from Jacob's entry into Egypt until his departure 430 years elapsed. And from the departure out of Egypt up to the building of Solomon's Temple, in the fourth year of his reign, 480 years passed. Finally, from the building of the Temple to Jesus Christ, according to the calculations of the Gospel writers, 490 years elapsed. And thus, by this reckoning derived from Holy Writ, I calculate 4,073 years eight months, more or less. Now from Jesus Christ until the era of the differing sects [*twentieth century*] I shall add nothing, for I have reckoned and calculated my present prophecies according to the rules of astronomic links, and by my natural instinct, and when, some time later, Saturn makes his revolution from 7 April to 25 August, Jupiter from 14 June to 7 October, Mars from 17 April to 22 May, Mercury from 3 to 24 February and from 25 September to 16 October, Saturn in Capricorn, Jupiter in Aquarius, Mars in Scorpio, Venus in Pisces, Mercury for a month in Capricorn, Aquarius, and Pisces, the Moon in Aquarius, the head of the Dragon [*Draco*] in Libra: its tail in its opposing sign following a Jupiter-Mercury conjunction, with a quadrant giving an aspect from Mars to Mercury, and the head of the Dragon will be with a Sun-Jupiter conjunction; the year will be peaceful and without eclipse, and then not so at all, for it will mark the beginning of a persecution of the Christian Church more widespread than anything that has been done in Africa; and that will correspond to the end of [*the monarchy*] which will last until the year 1792 [*21 September 1792: abolition of the French monarchy and proclamation of the Republic*], which will be thought to be a new era; after which the Roman people will start to rise up and chase some obscure shadows in order to find again their original verve [*Italian unity and the Risorgimento*], not without great divisions and continual changes [*of governments*].

Venice in great strength shall raise the wings of power so high that she shall not be too far removed from the power of Ancient Rome. And in that time a great Turkish fleet shall be allied with the Italians[1] [*in the partition of Greece*], with the help of the Russian power, which will prevent the two Greeces[2] [*Royalist and Venizelist*] from having the same objectives. The country where the ancient triumphal arches were built [*Italy*] shall be allied with England.

There will be a great disorder in the Adriatic [*the Balkan question which would trigger off the First World War, following the assassination at Sarajevo, Bosnia*]. There will then be great disorder in the Adriatic [*Northern Epirus, Italy, Albania, Bosnia*], when what was united is

---

[1] *Ligusticus sinus:* Gulf of Genoa. DHB.
[2] *Cretenses:* inhabitants of Crete, hence Greeks.

reduced to barely a single house [*burning of Smyrna by the Turks*], and the superpower[1] Germany[2] will be involved in the conflict around the 45th parallel [*Austro-Hungarian Empire, which would disappear during the First World War*] as well as the 41st, 42nd and 37th parallels.

After Italian unity, Rome will adopt a policy of conquest. Nostradamus focuses upon the Balkans question which led to the First World War. To do this, he will give the latitudes of the towns, areas and countries surrounding the Balkans, and which are to be the scene of bitter and bloody fighting. Thus the 37th parallel crosses the Cyclades, the Morea and Cilicia. The 41st crosses Macedonia and Thrace, via Istanbul, Salonica, Monastir, Evros and Stroumitza. The 42nd takes in Macedonia, Albania, Italy and Bulgaria, via Rome, Andrinopolis and Skopje. The 45th goes through Serbia, Bosnia and Italy, also Belgrade, Bucharest and Venice. Readers who wish to understand more of the geographical, historical and constitutional factors involved in the events leading to World War I, including the relevant Greek background, should turn to Professor Nicholas Svoronos' book, which excellently describes the Balkan crisis which preceded it.

After geographically situating the starting point of World War I, Nostradamus goes on to describe Hitler as the second Antichrist (after Nero).[3] Hitler is thus designated as much for his persecution of the Jews as for his persecution of Christians. After service during World War I as a corporal in the Austrian Army, from 1919 Hitler was a member of the German Socialist party.

And in this same time and in this region [*the Mesopotamia of Europe*] the infernal power [*Nazism*] will attack the Church of Jesus Christ, giving all power to the adversaries of Christian law; it shall be led by a second Antichrist [*Hitler*] who persecutes this Church and the Pope, with the help of goverments[4] which shall fall[5] and be seduced by speeches [*of Hitler*], through their ignorance, and who shall do worse than a madman armed with a sword [*persecution of the Jews*]. The power of this Antichrist will last only until the end of him who is born near the end of the age [*the twentieth century, principal aim of the prophecy; Hitler being born in 1889*] and until [*the liberation of*] Lyon,[6] allied with the chosen one of Modena [*Mussolini. The Modena region, with Ferrara and Bologna, were the key starting points of Fascism*], who will support him[7] [*his power once*]

[1] Cf. CX,Q100, Vol. I.
[2] The Mesopotamia of Europe: Germanic tribes between the Rhine and the Danube.
[3] Cf. CIX,Q17; CIX,Q53; CIX,Q76; CVI,Q67, all in Vol. I (pages 222, 223, 224 and 225 respectively).
[4] The Axis powers.
[5] Temporal, what passes with time, as opposed to eternal. DL.
[6] Cf. CIII,Q46, Vol. I.
[7] Latin *fulcire:* to support, sustain. D.LAT.

begun], through Ferrara, and he will keep himself in power from Liguria to the Adriatic, a little while after [*the invasion of*] Sicily.[1]

In 1921, prior to Mussolini's march on Rome, three towns in particular were important bastions of Fascism. On 3 April an extraordinarily well-attended demonstration took place at Bologna: 'The Festival of the Fascist Party'. A few days later, on 15 May, parliamentary elections were held. The Fascists scored a resounding victory: 35 candidates were elected, one of them being Benito Mussolini, who gained 172,491 votes at Bologna.[2] One of the main Fascist leaders was Italo Balbo of Ferrara.[1]

A year later, on 12 May 1922, Balbo flung his 40,000 troops into the conquest of Ferrara, then Rovigo and Bologna. The Fascist forces were also in action in Liguria.

At the start of September 1944, Lyon was liberated. One might ask why Nostradamus chose Lyon as the temporal reference point to mark the link between this town's liberation and the German Army's retreat in Italy behind the Gothic Line between Rimini and La Spezia, i.e. between Liguria and the Adriatic. There are two reasons. First, to indicate time: Lyon's liberation and the investment of the Gothic Line took place simultaneously. Secondly, because of the importance of Lyon in the history of the French Resistance. Robert Aron[3] wrote: 'On 28 August, the pincer movement began to operate from both sides. Paris, which had been liberated two days previously, was crossed by Allied divisions, some driving on deep into north-eastern France and Belgium, while others pushed towards Dijon. . . .The first objective was to be the link-up of the Allied forces in Provence with those in Normandy. To achieve this, they had to march on Lyon.

'Lyon, which with Dijon was to provide the mouse-trap in which the Wehrmacht could be caught, had since June 1940 played a vital role in France. As the centre of the Resistance, it also consequently became the capital of repression, terror and sometimes of discord. . . .' As for the persecution directed against the Catholic Church and its Pope by Hitler and Nazism, Hans Kuhner[4] wrote: 'The Concordat signed with Germany in 1933 was to the Nazi terror regime only a piece of paper and had been violated since its signature; shortly after it, a bloody persecution of Catholics began which lasted until the end of World War II. When Hitler came to Rome in 1938, the Pope refused to see the murderer of thousands of innocent people. He had the Vatican closed and left Rome conspicuously.'

★ ★ ★

[1] Trinacria, Sicily.
[2] The new Emilia was made up of the ancient provinces of Bologna, *Ferrara*, Forlì, Massa and Carrara, Modena, Parma, Piacenza, Ravenna and Reggio.
[3] HLFRA.
[4] DDP.

After reaching this point in his Letter to Henri, Nostradamus goes on to elaborate upon the Third World War and the Wars of the Antichrist (1999) waged by the Marxist regimes of the Soviet and Asiatic empires, allied with the Moslem countries.

Then Rome shall disappear.[1] The French Communist leader will be accompanied by a large number of people coming from the distant Soviet Empire which will impose the great law [*Communist*], and thus for some time the blood of the innocent shall be shed by the harmful[2] who will have risen up [*from their headquarters*]; then because of great revolutions[3] the things which keep memory [*books*] shall experience great losses, as will literature; and that shall be from the Russian side through divine will, and shall take place when once Satan is bound. Thus there will be a universal peace among men and the Church of Jesus Christ be delivered from all tribulation, after the inhabitants of Gaza[4] will have wished to mingle gall with honey by their infamous seduction, and that shall be close to the seventh millennium [*the year 2000*], so that Jesus Christ's sanctuary [*Jerusalem*] will no longer be trampled[5] by the feet of the unfaithful ones coming from Russia, the world approaching a great conflagration, although my calculations in my prophecies do not cover the whole course of time, which goes far further.

Nostradamus once again insists that his prophecy has a temporal limit – the seventh millennium.

In the letter I wrote some years ago, addressed to my son César, I quite clearly stated various points other than these presages. [*A summary of the method and thought behind the prophecies, as well as the origin of the latter and some cautions to the reader.*]

But here, Sire, I have included diverse great and marvellous events which our successors will see. And it is during this astrological calculation according to Holy Scripture that the persecution of the clergy shall begin, through the power of the Soviet Union united with the Orientals [*China?*]. And this persecution shall last just under eleven years and thus shall collapse the main leader of the Soviet Union [*Russia*]. When these eleven years have ended, its Southern ally [*the Moslem countries of the south: Iran, Syria, Iraq, Afghanistan, the Palestinians etc.*] will come to the fore to persecute the clergy even more violently, for three years, through a seductive apostasy, and via a person who shall derive absolute

---

[1] *Passer*: to die, disappear. DL7V.

[2] Latin *nocere*: to harm, be malevolent. D.LAT.

[3] Deluge, water, flood, whirlpool and typhoon are often used by Nostradamus to signify political upheavals or revolutionary movements.

[4] Azotos, in Greek, for Ashdod, one of the five Philistine towns. GAB. Nostradamus here denotes the Palestinians.

[5] Latin *conculcare:* to trample underfoot. D.LAT.

power from the militant Church [*Moslem fundamentalists?*], and the holy people of God who observe His Law and all religious orders shall be greatly persecuted and afflicted, so much so that the blood of the true ecclesiastics shall flow everywhere and one of these horrible temporal Rulers [*Iran?*] will receive such praise from his adherents that he shall spill more human blood of innocent churchmen than there is wine. And this leader shall commit unbelievable crimes against the Church, so that human blood runs in the streets and churches like heavy rain; and the rivers near us shall turn red with blood and the sea too will redden from a great naval war, so that it may be said of the relations between one head of state and another: naval battles have turned the sea's surface red. Then in this same year and during the following ones, there shall be the most horrible pestilence which will add to the preceding famine and such great tribulations will not have been known since the foundation of Christ's Church, and that will be throughout all regions of Italy. And it shall also leave its mark on all areas of Spain. Thus then the third leader of the Soviet Union, listening to the complaint of the people, and his main claim, will equip a very large army and cross the straits [*Bosphorus, Straits of Ormuz, Gulf of Aden*] which had been coveted by his forefathers and great-grandfathers [*cf. the Will of Peter the Great*], to reclaim it for his state, then the great Capetian shall be restored to his original state; but in the end, his reign shall be desolated and all abandoned, so that the destruction of the Saints of Saints [*Rome*] shall occur through paganism. The Old and New Testaments shall be forbidden and burned, after which the Antichrist shall be the infernal prince; and for the last time all the Christian countries shall tremble and also because of the unfaithful ones[1] [*the Moslems*], for twenty-five years,[2] there shall be wars and battles still more ruinous, and towns, villages, castles and other buildings shall be burned, laid waste or destroyed, with a great flood of the blood of young girls, married women, violated widows, suckling infants thrown against the walls of towns, dashed[3] thus and bruised; and so many misfortunes will be provoked by Satan, Prince of Darkness, that almost all the planet will be in chaos and laid waste. After this time, which men shall find long, the peace of the earth shall be renewed through the coming of the Golden Age. God the Creator, hearing the affliction of His people, shall order Satan to be bound and cast into the abyss of Hell,[4] into the deepest pit: thus shall commence a universal peace between God and men, and Satan shall remain bound for about a

[1] Cf. CVIII,Q96, Vol. I, and CIX,Q83.
[2] Cf. CVIII,Q77, Vol. I.
[3] Latin *allidere:* to hit. D.LAT.
[4] Latin *barathrum:* Hell. D.LAT.

thousand years, which will bring a greater strength to the power of the Church; and then he will once again be released.

All these outlines are in accord with the Holy Scriptures and things visible in the sky [*astronomy*], namely Saturn, Jupiter and Mars and other planets in conjunction, as one can see in more detail in certain quatrains. I could have made more detailed calculations and matched some against others, but considering, O Most Serene King, that censorship might bring certain difficulties, I have therefore withdrawn my pen from the paper during the calm of my nights. Indeed, O Most Powerful Ruler of all things, many happenings to come are clearly expressed with good sense and conciseness, but I neither wished nor was able to assemble them all in this letter to you; for in order to understand certain events, it is necessary for a little of destiny to be accomplished; and so that your dignity and humanity may be great throughout the earth, as well as your piety towards God, show yourself worthy of being the only one to bear the name of very powerful and most Christian King which the authority of all religion shall grant you.

But what I wish most fervently, O most clement King, is that through your unequalled and wise humanity you reflect upon my heartfelt desire and complete intention of obeying your serenest Majesty, since my vision has made me see your solar splendour [*reference to Bourbon origins*], a greatness to which my work, for all its importance, does not aspire.

Salon, this 27 June 1558.

NOSTRADAMUS AS HISTORIAN

SUBJECTS OF THE QUATRAINS AND SIXAINS

Moorish Revolt in Granada, 1567 – Their Expulsion from Spain, 1610

The Thirty Years War, 1618–48 – Gaston of Orleans in Lorraine, 1630

The Secret Marriage of Gaston of Orleans to Marguerite of Lorraine

Wallenstein and the Thirty Years' War, 1618–34 – His Treachery and Execution with His Accomplices, 1634

Marie de Medici's Exile to the Spanish Low Countries – Her Death, 1642

Charles I of England Driven from Power, 1649 – Cromwell Becomes Protector, 1653

William III against Louis XIV's France, 1672–1702 – The War of the League of Augsburg, 1688–97

The Duke of Anjou as King of Spain, 1700 – The War of the Spanish Succession, 1701–14

The Farnese Succession in Italy, 1732–33 – Don Carlos, Son of Philip V, King of Spain

The French Revolution, Cause of Napoleon's Accession – The Oath of the Tennis Court, 20 June 1789 – The National Assembly, 17 June 1789 – The Royal Family Imprisoned, 10 August 1792

War between France, Germany and Spain, 1795 – The Fall of the Republican System

The First Italian Campaign, 1796–97 – Napoleon at Villanova, Cremona and Mantua

The Egyptian Campaign, 1798 – Bonaparte's Administration of the Country

Masséna in Genoa, May 1800 – The Defeat of the Imperial Army – The Besieged Eat Oat Bread

Seven Years of War for the Milanese, 1792–1800 – Napoleon in Milan, 2 June 1800

18 Brumaire – Bonaparte and His Two Brothers – The French Army on the Var

Napoleon Emperor Thanks to His Victories – Louis XVII Welcomed by the Vatican – Coalitions against Napoleon

Louis XVI, Madame Elizabeth, Louis XVII and His Sister in the Temple – The False Dauphins and the Bourbon Characteristics

Napoleon's Military Coup against the Quirinal, 6 July 1809 - Rebellion in Rome and the Campagna – Failure of Conscription

The Beresina, November 1812 – The Grand Army between the Dniepr and the Dwina

Preparation for the Return from Elba, 1815 – Napoleon and His Old Comrades-in-Arms

Napoleon and the Return from Elba, 1 March 1815 – The Treachery of Marie-Louise, September 1814

The Battle of Navarino, October 1827 – Greek Independence, February 1830

The War of Greek Independence, 1821–28 – Chios, Tripolis, Navarino, Trebizond

War in Piedmont – Mortara, March 1849 – Defeat of Mortara before that of Novara

Garibaldi from Sicily and Naples to Rome, 1860–67 – The Agreement between Garibaldi and the British – The Shortcomings of Francis II, King of the Two Sicilies

End of the Pope's Temporal Power, 1870 – Role of the Secret Societies – Internal Struggles

Garibaldi in Brazil, 1835 – The Hohenzollern Candidacy to the Spanish Throne – The Duke of Aosta as King of Spain, 1870 – Garibaldi's Landing at Marseille, 1870 – The Advent of the Third Republic

The Succession to the Spanish Throne a Cause of the Franco-Prussian War of 1870 – French Troops Surrounded at Metz – The Eastern Army at Villersexel – 1830–70: Forty Years of War – 1871–1914: Forty Years of Peace

The Russian Revolution Leads to Famine and Disaster, 1917 – Human Rights Ignored – Battles of the Somme, 1916–18

The First World War Follows the Belle Epoque – Progress in Travel by Land, Sea and Air – Twentieth-century Wars

The Russo-German Pact, 23 August 1939 – The German Wheat Shortage, 1939

Mussolini and Clara Petacci Taken by Lorry to Milan – The Seven Corpses at Piazzale Loreto in Milan, 29 April 1945

Hesitation over the Provence Landing, August–December 1943 – The German Occupation as Far as Monaco – Imprisonment of Mussolini – Mussolini Hanged in Milan, 29 April 1945

The Link-up between the French, American, British and Russian Armies on the Danube, April–May 1945 – Mussolini in a Van and the Fall of Hitler, 29 April 1945

Socialism and François Mitterrand – The First Steps in the Rise to Power

Nostradamus' Prophecy Carried Worldwide by the Media, 1981

The Prophecy of Nostradamus Attacked by the Clergy, 1981

Moorish Revolt in Granada, 1567.
Their Expulsion from Spain, 1610

Par les contrées du grand fleuve Bétique,[1]
Loin d'Ibère[2] au royaume de Grenade[3]
Croix repoussées par gens Mahométiques,
Un de Cordube[4] trahira[5] la fin contrade.[6]

CIII, Q20

Interpretation

Across the regions bordering on the Guadalquivir, from as far as the Ebro to the Kingdom of Granada, the Mohammedans will drive back [conversion to] the Cross. Finally they shall be driven out of Cordoba and the country.

History

'Already masters of all the Eastern Mediterranean, the Turkish vessels indulged in piracy between France and Italy. . . . *The Moors of Granada*, supported by Constantinople, whence they received subsidies and arms, revolted in 1567 and were only crushed by a bloody war, part guerrilla combat, part pitched battles, won by Don John of Austria, Philip II's half-brother, to whom he had entrusted the command. In order to avoid further insurrections and to reduce the vulnerability of the coastline to Turkish attacks, Philip II ordered the transportation of Granada's Moors to central Spain. Resettled in *Estremadura* [Cordova], La Mancha, Old Castile and Galicia, they returned as labourers to those provinces their ancestors had occupied as conquerors seven centuries earlier.

From Oran, their furthest eastern stronghold, the turbanned corsairs harassed solitary Spanish ships and ransacked coastal villages. . . .Local help and contacts were not lacking, and this support was particularly strong in Spain *between Algeciras[7] and the mouth of the Ebro [D'Ibère au royaume de Grenade]*.

An internal political decision, the most important of his reign, was to add to the stagnation. This was *the expulsion of the Moors. . . .The considerable efforts made* since Philip II *to convert them had failed. [Croix repoussées par gens Mahométiques]*. . . .In 1609 and 1610 royal edicts forbade their *leaving their allotted territory [trahira contrade]*.' [8]

[1] Guadalquivir (from the Arab Oued-al-Kebir, *the great river*), the *Boetis* of the ancients, runs through Adujar and Cordova. DHB. This river flows north of the Betic Cordillera.

[2] Iberus, now the Ebro: Spanish river. DHB.

[3] Founded by the Moors in the tenth century. Originally part of the Kingdom of *Cordova*. DHB.

[4] Cordoue, Corduba, i.e. Cordova, town in Spain on right bank of the Guadalquivir. DHB.

[5] Latin *trahere:* to take by force. D.LAT.

[6] Or *contrede*, early form of *contrée* (region/area). DAFL.

[7] Town 1km from Gibraltar, south-west of Granada. AVL.

[8] HDEJP.

The Thirty Years' War, 1618–48.
Gaston of Orleans in Lorraine, 1630

Dedans Hongrie par Boheme, Navarre,[1]
Et par Bannieres painctes[2] seditions:
Par fleurs de lys pays portant la barre,[3]
Contre Orléans fera esmotions.

CV, Q89

Interpretation

In Hungary, because of Bohemia, and also in Navarre, there will be deceptive seditions which will occupy [the King of France] and Navarre, who will revolt in Lorraine against Gaston of Orleans.

History

'It was the *Bohemian* revolt which led to the Thirty Years' War. It began spontaneously on 23 May 1618 with the famous defenestration of Prague. . . .

A French intervention helped the imperial cause far more than was Louis XIII's ministers' intention. At the start of the winter, Ferdinand had sent the Prince of Fürstenberg to Paris as his ambassador, to ask the devoutly Christian king for his aid in conquering the heretics. He emphasized the danger which would threaten the Church were the Protestants to triumph in *Bohemia*. The pious Louis XIII was swayed by this. He too had to combat rebellious subjects, the Calvinists of the *Béarn* region, ever since he had undertaken to re-establish Catholicism in their territory. It was natural that he should make the connection between *Béarnais resistance* to the royal edict and *the Bohemian revolt*. . . .

The two main armies met near Prague. The King of Bohemia's army was comprised of a very few Czechs, but numerous Germans from all regions, Austrians, *Hungarians*, and even Englishmen. . . .

In 1629, on the occasion of a disagreement over the Bishopric of Metz, the Emperor had installed garrisons in two dependent towns, Vic and Moyenvic, while in 1630 the King of France had affirmed his sovereignty by extending over the Three Bishoprics the powers of a judicial intendant. . . . It was far easier for Richelieu to find a pretext to intervene in Lorraine, since Duke Charles IV had taken a distinctly hostile line towards Louis XIII. When, after the Day of Dupes and Marie de Medici's flight to Brussels,[4] Gaston of Orleans in his turn left the kingdom, it was to Nancy, close to the Duke of *Lorraine*, that he withdrew, and the rumour quickly circulated that *the Duke supported the betrothal of Monsieur to Marguerite of Lorraine*, his sister. The King of France could hardly allow the imperial troops to be installed permanently at Vic and Moyenvic, so near to Metz. In December 1631 a French army besieged Moyenvic and seized the town. Charles IV thus had to accept an agreement which became the Treaty of Vic, signed on 6 January 1632. He ceded the fortress of Marsal, north-east of Nancy, to the King of France; allowed the French troops unrestricted movement through his duchy; and undertook to abstain henceforth from all *intelligences, leagues, associations, and frequentation* that he had or might have with any Prince or State prejudicial to the King's cause, States, and territory under his allegiance or protection [*fainctes seditions*].'⁵

¹ Province forming part of the Béarn-et-Navarre district. DHB.
² Banners or standards being raised implied open hostility: the nobility was often 'up in arms', flags flying, against Richelieu. DL7V.
³ Barrois, ancient area of France within Lorraine. DL7V. The arms of Lorraine were composed of a bar.
⁴ Cf. cIX,Q78.
⁵ LGDTA.

The Secret Marriage of Gaston of Orleans to Marguerite of Lorraine

Dame à l'absence de son grand capitaine,
Sera priée¹ d'amour du Viceroy:²
Faincte promesse et malheureuse estreine,³
Entre les mains du grand Prince Barroys.

CVII,Q9

Interpretation

The Lady [Marie de Medici] in the absence of her great captain [Gaston of Orleans, Lieutenant of the Realm] will be invited to share the tender overtures engineered by the viceroy [Charles IV, Duke of Lorraine] which are to be made through a secret promise and because of an unfortunate fate; this having been arranged by the great Lorrainian Prince [Charles IV].

History

Cf. The historical texts quoted after the preceding quatrain.
    'But in order to take the necessary precautions on the Rhine, the French troops' route from Champagne through Lorraine into Alsace had first to be opened. The situation of Lorraine, between the Kingdom of France and the Empire, thus became greatly confused, for the term Lorraine was itself only a geographical one. To the west, the region of Bar-le-Duc, called the "*Barrois* Mouvant" was in the domain of the King of France: i.e. its Duke was *vassal to the King*. . . .'⁴

¹ To ask, invite. DL7V.
² Head of a state dependent on a kingdom or other state. DL7V.
³ Early form of *étrenne*, meaning luck or fortune. DAFL.
⁴ LGDTA.

Wallenstein and the Thirty Years War, 1618–34. His Treachery and Execution with his Accomplices, 1634

Un capitaine¹ de la grand Germanie,²
Se viendra rendre par simulé secours:
Au Roy des Roys ayde de Pannonie,³
Que sa révolte fera de sang grand cours.

CIX,Q90

Interpretation

An army commander from great Germany will falsely bring support to the Emperor-King aided by Hungary. And his revolt will cause much blood to flow.

History

'Albert of Wallenstein *entered the service* of Ferdinand⁴ during the Duke of Styria's war against Venice. In 1618, at the beginning of the Thirty Years War, he was thirty-five. He had formed and was *commanding* a regiment in Moravia [*un capitaine*]. *He took the King's side* when Moravia declared support for the rebels.

Maximilian thought Wallenstein was in agreement with the King of Spain in wanting to give the House of Hapsburg "universal Monarchy" [*Roy des Roys*].

Disagreements between Wallenstein and the Archduke Ferdinand became more pronounced.

Richelieu was redoubling diplomatic activity in Germany, seizing every opportunity that chance might present him with. One such occasion was Wallenstein's treason. . . . The initial overtures made by Wallenstein to the Emperor's enemies reached France very early on.

Wallenstein summoned the senior officers of his army on 11 January 1634 at Pilsen for a council of war. The Emperor had knowledge of this meeting and was in no doubt as to Wallenstein's intentions: what was being planned could only be an attempt by the *commander in chief* [*capi-*

taine] to organize an officers' *plot* against the Emperor and to persuade
the entire army to throw in its lot with him. . . . The drama unfolded
on the evening of 24 February, in two distinct acts. The first was a
banquet to which were invited Wallenstein's closest henchmen: Trcka,
Kinsky and two senior officers, Ilow and Niemann. The banquet had
scarcely ended before the officers in charge of the executions admitted
the dragoons, who at once slaughtered Kinsky and Ilow. Trcka managed
to escape from the room but was killed by musket shots in the courtyard.
Niemann met a similar fate and the *massacre* was complete. The second
act was even grimmer. Wallenstein had remained on his sickbed, unaware
of what had happened. After a brief deliberation the officers decided to
kill him too, although he was in no fit state to defend himself.'[5]

[1] General term for head of an army, senior commander: Alexander, Hannibal, Caesar,
Napoleon I etc. are some of the greatest 'captains' in history. DL7V.
[2] See any map of the (Holy Roman – in effect German) Empire during the seventeenth
century.
[3] Pannonia: European region between Norica and Dacia (Hungary). D.LAT.
[4] Ferdinand II was crowned King of Bohemia in 1617, *King of Hungary* in 1618, and
Emperor in 1619. This monarch's generals were Maximilian of Bavaria, Tilly and
Wallenstein. DHB.
[5] LGDTA.

Marie de Medici's Exile to the Spanish Low Countries. Her Death, 1642

> La dame Grecque de beauté laydique,[1]
> Heureuse faicte de proces[2] inumérable:
> Hors translatée au règne Hispanique,
> Captive, prinse mourir mort misérable.
>
> CIX,Q78

Interpretation

The lady who is as beautiful as the Greek courtesan Laïs [Marie de
Medici] will be happy until she indulges in numerous quarrels. She shall
leave [France] in order to surrender to the kingdom of Spain [the Spanish
Low Countries]. Imprisoned, arrested, she will die wretchedly.

History

'Marie de Medici,[3] daughter of Francis I, Grand Duke of Tuscany, was *a remarkable beauty*. . . . Named Regent after Henri IV's death in 1610, she was only interested in destroying what that great king had achieved. . . .When she had succeeded in giving Richelieu administrative power (1624) she started *perpetual intrigues* against him. She accused him of ingratitude because he would not sacrifice the interests of France for her.

She tried, but failed, to have Richelieu disgraced [The Day of Dupes, 12 November 1630]. *Arrested*, she managed to escape and reached the *Low Countries*, where she died destitute.'[4]

[1] Greek: Λαΐς, -ϊδος, Lais.DG. Greek courtesan celebrated for her wit and beauty, born at Hycara in *Sicily*. DHB. Nostradamus here alludes to the Greeks populating Italy.
[2] Figurative: quarrel. DL7V.
[3] Ancient Guelph family of Florence. When she attained supreme power, there was much talk of her *distant and brilliant origins*.DL7V.
[4] DHB.

Charles I of England Driven from Power, 1649. Cromwell Becomes Protector, 1653

> Pour ne vouloir consentir au divorce,
> Qui puis après sera connu indigne:
> Le Roy des Isles sera chassé par force,
> Mis à son lieu qui de Roy n'aura signe.

CX,Q22

Interpretation

Because of his refusal to divorce, the King of the [British] Isles shall be declared unworthy [of governing] and driven out of power by force [execution]; a person who will not have the title of king shall be set in his place.

History

'Charles I, whose family life was blameless, lacked intuition and was reputedly influenced by *his wife*[1] and his favourites of the moment. This explained the growing opposition to absolute monarchy. . . .'[2]

'The Protestants rebelled and drew up the famous Covenant, whereby they undertook to defend their faith to the death [1638]. Charles, unable to silence them, was obliged to summon a new Parliament in 1640. But this Parliament set itself up *in judgement over his behaviour* [*connu indigne*], condemned his chief minister, Strafford, to death, and formed an army to oppose him, led by Essex and Cromwell. The royal troops were *beaten* in various encounters [*par force*]. . . . Charles I, who had taken refuge in Scotland, was handed over to the rebels by the Scots [1647]. Brought before Parliament, he was condemned to death as a tyrant and executed in 1649.

Oliver Cromwell proclaimed a Republic. Four years later he was recognized as Head of State under the title of *Protector* [*de Roy n'aura signe*]. From that time on, Cromwell ruled as *absolute sovereign.*'[3]

[1] The king had married Henrietta of France, daughter of Henri IV and sister of Louis XIII.
[2] HRU.
[3] DHB.

William III against Louis XIV's France, 1672–1702. The War of the League of Augsburg, 1688–97

> L'aisné vaillant de la fille du Roy,[1]
> Repoussera si profond les Celtiques,
> Qu'il mettra foudres,[2] combien en tel arroy[3]
> Peu et loing, puis profond es Hesperiques.[4]
>
> CIV,Q99

Interpretation

The courageous elder son [William III] of the daughter of the king [Charles I] will drive back the French so far that he will put them in great disarray through his forceful actions, not numerous but far-reaching, then deep into Spain.

History

'William was elected Stathouder of Holland in 1672, with the title of Prince of Orange, and led the Republic's troops in the war against Louis XIV. Although often defeated in this war, he fought the enemy on every front and more than proved his *courage*, prudence and skill, concluding with France the honourable Peace of Nijmegen, which assured the independence of the United Provinces in 1678.'[5]

'The Treaties of Ryswick which ended the War of the League of Augsburg were signed on 20 September and 30 October 1697. Louis XIV recognized William III as King of England, gave back Catalonia to *Spain,* and in the Low Countries surrendered Mons, Courtrai and Charleroi. He returned to the Duke of Lorraine territories occupied since his reign began; to the Emperor, Philipsburg, Brisach, Freiburg and Trier; and to Sweden, the Principality of Deux-Ponts. This eleven-year war drained the country, and finances were shaky. While it left Louis XIV's prestige undimmed, it increased British power dangerously. The House of Commons, indeed, was to thank William III "for the honour he had given back to England of holding the balance of Europe".

On 16 September 1701, King James II of England died at St Germain. Louis XIV immediately recognized as James's successor his son, under the title of "James III". The instant consequence of this was to give William III a pretext for declaring war. In fact, on 7 September William III had signed with Holland and the Empire *the Grand Alliance against France.* In 1703, the war was to become general.

On 19 March 1702, William of Orange, King of England and *Louis XIV's implacable enemy,* died from injuries received after falling from his horse. . . . The Grand Alliance was not affected by his death. "It was so well established," said St-Simon, "that William's spirit continued to animate it." '[6]

---

[1] William III, born in 1650 at The Hague, was the son of William II of Nassau, Prince of Orange, and of Henrietta Maria Stuart, *daughter of Charles I, King of England.* DHB

[2] Powerful effect, having a violent quality to its energy. DL7V.

[3] For *désarroy,* by aphesis.

[4] Hesperia, the name originally given by the Greeks to Italy, was then used to refer to Spain, when Greek geographical knowledge extended further west. DHB.

[5] DHB.

[6] L.XIV.JR.

The Duke of Anjou as King of Spain, 1700. The War of the Spanish Succession, 1701–14

Nul de l'Espagne, mais de l'antique France,
Ne sera esleu pour le tremblant nacelle[1]
A l'ennemy sera faicte fiance,
Qui dans son regne sera peste cruelle.

                                                    CV,Q49

Interpretation

A king of ancient France and not of Spain shall be chosen by a tottering power. There will be trust in yesterday's enemy [France]. And under his reign there will be a cruel calamity.

History

'Charles II: *the agony of Spain*. As if he wished to symbolize in his own person *a dying Spain*, Charles II was sickly and melancholy. . . . It was this *diminished* Spain which had to confront a France at the summit of her power. . . . Exhausted and dispirited, King Charles II bequeathed his crown to the claimant who, since he was the strongest, had the best chance of keeping his enormous inheritance united. This was Philip of Anjou, grandson of Louis XIV [*de l'antique France*].'[2]

'The War of the Spanish Succession was to last thirteen years. It was *the longest and most terrible* of Louis XIV's reign. It was waged simultaneously in *Spain*, Italy, Germany, the Low Countries, and eastern and northern France. . . . The Peace of Utrecht was signed in 1713. Philip V was to keep Spain and her colonies, formally renouncing all his claims to the French throne. . . . The War of the Spanish Succession had been futile and *ruinous* [*peste cruelle*]: France had not profited in any way from this enterprise, and had also forfeited her dominance in Europe; *she had been drained of blood and money*.'[3]

---

[1] Latin *navicella*, diminutive of *navis*, vessel. Symbolically speaking, the craft on which one is supposed to travel through the vicissitudes of life (depicted as a 'sea'). DL7V. Appropriate image denoting Spain, surrounded as she is by sea from Irun past Gibraltar to Barcelona.
[2] HEFDP.
[3] HFAM.

The Farnese Succession in Italy, 1732–33. Don Carlos, Son of Philip V, King of Spain

Par[1] car[2] Nersaf,[3] à ruine grande discorde,
Ne l'un ne l'autre n'aura election:
Nersaf du peuple aura amour et concorde,
Ferrare[4] Collonne[5] grande protection.

CVIII,Q67

Interpretation

There will be a great, ruinous discord between the Duke of Parma on the one side and Don Carlos and Elizabeth Farnese on the other. Neither the one [Duke of Parma] nor the other [Elizabeth Farnese] will be chosen. Don Carlos [the Farnese heir] shall have love and concord and be protected in the Papal States.

History

'The Spanish Succession in Italy had scarcely been settled before the issue of the Duchy of Parma and Piacenza provoked dissension and intrigue. Francis,[6] *Duke of Parma*, had as heirs one brother, Antonio, aged forty-five and grotesquely obese, who was not expected to live long, and one daughter, Elizabeth, who was married to King Philip V of Spain. It was obvious that the Duchy would revert to Elizabeth, and the Emperor of Germany was prepared to recognize the claims of *Don Carlos*, one of Philip's sons. . . . The old rivalry between the Houses of Hapsburg and Bourbon was thus reawakened in Italy. . . . The Emperor ordered the Governor of Milan to enter the Duchy and assert his rights of suzerainty. For his part the King of Spain sent six thousand troops commanded by his son Don Carlos into Tuscany. . . . At the start of 1733, in the north, Villars and Charles Emmanuel I, King of Sardinia, invaded the Milan region and promptly took possession of it. In the south, Don Carlos first drove the Duke of Modena from his territories and advanced *across the Papal States* to attack the Kingdom of Naples. The Imperial Viceroy, Visconti, left without assistance, had to give in, and *Don Carlos' march was a triumph*. The Neapolitans, happy to have a king of their own, ran enthusiastically ahead of Don Carlos, opened their towns to him one after the other, and ceremonially proclaimed him King of the Two Sicilies on 10 May. Capua and Gaeta, which the Viceroy wanted to defend, each capitulated swiftly. The following year Don Carlos, at the head of a considerable fleet, sailed from Naples towards

Palermo, where he was crowned with *the same speed and rejoicing* [*amour et concorde*].' [7]

[1] For Parma, by apocope.
[2] For Carlos, by apocope.
[3] Anagram of Farnes(e). Most commentators have read this word as an anagram of France.
[4] Town south-east of Parma. AVL. Papal State.
[5] Town east of Rome. AVL. Papal State.
[6] Francis Farnese, Duke of Parma (1694–1727). DHB.
[7] HIIZ.

The French Revolution, Cause of Napoleon's Accession.
The Oath of the Tennis Court, 20 June 1789.
The National Assembly, 17 June 1789.
The Royal Family Imprisoned, 10 August 1792

Enfans sans mains[1] jamais veu si grand foudre,[2]
L'enfant Royal au jeu doesteuf[3] blessé,[4]
Au puy[5] brises[6] fulgures[7] allant mouldre,
Trois sous les chaines par le milieu troussées.[8]

CI,Q65

Interpretation

One will never have seen a child, without parental authority, become so great a war leader, when the royal child [Louis XVII] is affected by the Oath of the Tennis Court, [the king], through having wished to suppress the Assembly, will unleash thunderbolts [from the people] by going [to play] baker; three years later he will be taken away from the centre [power] and imprisoned.

History

'Napoleon was ten. . . . It was not enough to be a good pupil to obtain subsidy: your parents had to prove they lacked *sufficient resources*. Marboeuf attested to their poverty, declaring that the Bonapartes, with three children, had no money.

On 17 June 1789, the States-General became known as the National *Assembly*. This change of name was vitally significant.

On 23 June the King made his declaration to the States-General. . . .
The monarch began by *quashing and annulling* as illegal and unconstitut-
ional the resolution of the seventeenth, the one whereby the States-
General would henceforth be called the National Assembly.

The women who preceded the royal coach as it entered Paris were
displaying various *flours* to the multitude, and pointing towards the king
and his family, shouting: "Don't worry, friends, we won't be short of
bread any longer. We're bringing you the baker, the baker's wife and
the little baker's boy" [*allant mouldre*].' [9]

From 17 June 1789 to 10 August 1792, the date of the Royal Family's
incarceration in the Temple Prison, is a period of three years.

[1] Latin *manus:* authority, power; paternal authority in particular. DL.
[2] 'Napoleon was a great military leader.' DL7V. Cf.CII,Q76; CIII,Q13; CIV,Q43; and CIV,Q54 all Vol. I.
[3] *Esteuf:* term for the ball used for tennis. DAFL.
[4] *Atteindre:* to hit, wound. DL7V.
[5] Certain assemblies in ancient times were held on *puys* or hillocks. DAFL.
[6] *Briser:* to destroy, suppress. DL7/FV.
[7] Latin *fulger:* thunderbolt. DL.
[8] To carry off, take away. DAFL.
[9] HFA.

War between France, Germany and Spain, 1795. The Fall of the Republican System

Un an devant le conflict Italique,
Germains, Gaulois, Espagnols pour le fort,
Cherra l'escolle maison de république,
Où hors mis peu, seront suffoquez mors.

CII,Q39

Interpretation

A year before the Italian campaign, Germans, Frenchmen and Spaniards
will try their strength, then the republican teaching will collapse, except
for some who will be killed and suffocated.

History

'Treaties of Basle and The Hague. The French victories and Polish
affairs led in 1795 to an initial disruption of the coalition. *The King of*

Prussia was anxious not to let Russia and Austria proceed separately towards a third partition of Poland, and the *King of Spain*, threatened with *a French invasion*, signed the Peace of Basle [April 1795]. Prussia recognized the occupation by French forces of the territories on the left bank of the Rhine, and in Belgium and the other Imperial domains. The King of Spain surrendered Spanish San Domingo in the Antilles.'

'The Italian campaign lasted one year, from April 1796 to April 1797.' [April 1795–April 1796 – one year before the Italian campaign.]

Conspiracies. Bonaparte's dictatorship had created numerous malcontents among both the republican generals and the disappointed royalists. Several plots were hatched against the usurper. . . . In August 1803, a former *Chouan* leader, Georges Cadoudal, at the head of a band of determined followers, had schemed to attack and kill the First Consul and his escort. . . . The conspiracy was unmasked in January 1804. . . . The Duke of Enghien, a suspected conspirator, was taken to Vincennes, brought before a military tribunal, sentenced and shot. Shortly afterwards Cadoudal was guillotined, and Pichegru strangled [*suffoqué*] in his house. Moreau was exiled.

Cadoudal's conspiracy hastened the transformation of the Consulate into an hereditary monarchy. On 18 May 1804, a *senatus-consultum* established that *the government of the Republic* was entrusted to the Emperor Napoleon.[1]

[1] HFAM.

The First Italian Campaign, 1796–97. Napoleon at Villanova, Cremona and Mantua

A cité neuve[1] pensif pour condamner,
L'oisel de proye[2] au Ciel[3] se vient offrir:
Après victoire à captifs pardonner,
Crémone et Mantoue grand maux aura souffert.

CI,Q24

Interpretation

At Villanova no one will think further of condemning Bonaparte who will make offers to the Church. After his victory he will give proof of his clemency towards the prisoners. The towns of Cremona and Mantua will have suffered much.

History

'The next morning Bonaparte took up the pursuit again, making for Vicenza. Once he had reached the Brenta–Verona road, by way of *Villanova*, he entrusted the cavalry alone with the task of pursuing the enemy, and considered returning to Verona by the *Villanova* and Caldiero road, in order to come to Vaubois' aid. . . . When the inhabitants of Verona saw this handful of men who had previously left as fugitives through the Milan gate now return through the Venice gate as victors, they were astonished. *Neither friends nor enemies could contain their admiration.* From that time on, no one ever feared that the French might be driven out of Italy.'

'Bonaparte now faced the River Adda, which could not, like the Ticino, be skirted, because he would only have had to cross the Po at *Cremona*. . . . Serrurier's and Laharpe's divisions had been left at Pizzighettone, Lodi, *Cremona* and Cassano, to guard the Adda.'

'Bonaparte had scarcely signed the capitulation of *Mantua*, when he departed without waiting for Marshal Würmser to parade before him, and arrived at Bologna *to lay down the law to the Pope*.'

Bonaparte assembled *the prisoners* taken that day along the banks of the Senio, and spoke to them in Italian. These unfortunates imagined that their throats were going to be cut. Bonaparte reassured them, announcing to their great astonishment that he *was setting them free* provided they would then enlighten their compatriots as to *the intentions of the French, who had not come to destroy religion or the Holy See*, but wished only to dismiss the bad counsellors surrounding the Pope.' [4]

[1] Villanova: i.e. *cité neuve*, new city.
[2] The Napoleonic eagle.
[3] Used with capital letter to denote the Catholic Church.
[4] HDRAT, Vol. 2.

The Egyptian Campaign, 1798. Bonaparte's Administration of the Country

Combien de fois prinse Cité solaire[1],
Seras changeant les loix barbares et vaines:[2]
Ton mal s'approche. Plus seras tributaire,
Le Grand Hadrie recouvrira tes veines.[3]

CI,Q8

Interpretation

How many times shall the town of Cairo be taken, where the worthless Moslem laws shall be changed. Your misfortune approaches. You shall pay yet another tribute. Starting from the Adriatic the great personage [i.e. Bonaparte] will seize your wealth.

History

'Cairo was *taken* by the Turks in 1517, by the French in 1798, and by the English in 1801, when it was immediately returned to the Porte [Turkey].'[4]

'It was in Italy, while thinking about the Levant, that he first conceived the idea of the famous expedition launched the following year. "It is in Egypt," he wrote, "that England must be attacked." [Letter of 16 August 1797]. To attain his ends, he had summoned Admiral Brueys in the *Adriatic*, with six warships, several frigates and a few corvettes. . . .

The army had succeeded in landing; it was now necessary to create at Alexandria an administration in line with the customs of the country, and to halt an invasion plan to seize Egypt. . . .

Bonaparte made arrangements to establish French authority in Alexandria, then to leave the Delta and seize *Cairo*, capital of Egypt. . . . Bonaparte established a divan at Cairo as he had done at Alexandria. This divan, or municipal council, was to help him win over the Egyptians. It was agreed that similar ones were to be set up in all the provinces, and that these special divans would send deputies to the Cairo divan, which would thus be a great national divan [*changeant les lois barbares*].'[5]

'On 21 October 1798, Cairo rebelled: a terrible outbreak, which cost some 250 French lives, including that of the Governor of Cairo, General Dupuy. *The reprisals were as dreadful* as they were discreet [*ton mal s'approche*]. The work of pacification and *organization* was more remarkable: all the necessary resources [*tributaire*] for the army had to be collected, and this in a wretchedly poor country.'[6]

---

[1] Heliopolis, i.e. City of the Sun, 11 km north-east of Cairo. On 20 March 1800 Kléber won a resounding victory there over the Turks. DHB.

[2] Latin *vanus*: worthless. DLLB.

[3] Symbolic: wealth, resources to be used. DL7V.

[4] DHB.

[5] HDRAT.

[6] NEE.

Masséna in Genoa, May 1800. The Defeat of the Imperial Army. The Besieged Eat Oat Bread

Le conducteur de l'armée françoise,
Cuidant perdre le principal phalange:
Par sus pavé de l'avaigne[1] et d'ardoise,[2]
Soy parfondra[3] par Gennes gent estrange.

CVII,Q39

Interpretation

The leader of the French army [Napoleon], thinking his principal army [Masséna] lost, when on the street bread made from oats and slates will be eaten, shall in Genoa trouble the strangers [Austrians].

History

'If Napoleon could have emerged into Italy, he would already have seized the *Austrian* general [*gent estrange*] and snatched him away from the walls of Genoa. Others were claiming that Bonaparte *the general had deemed the Ligurian army a necessary sacrifice* [*cuidant perdre le principal phalange*] in a major operation. The Genoese and our own soldiers themselves considered that they had been sacrificed to the glory of France.

Masséna's fortitude held out to the very end. Before surrendering, the soldiers were saying, he would have them eat their very boots; a dismal sort of bread, made with *oats* and beans, had been devoured also. . . . *The streets* [*sus pavé*] were littered with unhappy wretches dying of starvation.

Thus ended the memorable siege, during which *a French army* had distinguished itself by great devotion and heroism. It had taken more prisoners and killed more enemy soldiers than it numbered in its own ranks. With 15,000 men, it had captured or disposed of 18,000 *Austrians* [*gent estrange*]. Above all, it had destroyed the morale [*parfondra*] of the [Austrian Imperial] army by compelling it to make constant and extraordinary efforts. But at what price had this brave garrison of *Genoa* achieved such things? . . . Soult, the second in command, remained in enemy hands. . . .'[4]

[1] Latin *avena:* oats. D.LAT.
[2] They made bread from chopped-up straw, writes D'Aubigné in *Histoire Universelle.*
[3] Latin *perfundere:* to distress, disturb. D.LAT.
[4] HDEAT.

Seven Years of War for the Milanese, 1792–1800.
Napoleon in Milan, 2 June 1800

Devant cité de l'Insubre[1] contrée,
Sept ans sera le siège devant mis:
Le très grand Roy y fera son entrée,
Cité puis libre hors de ses ennemis.

CVII,QI5

Interpretation

Milan and the Milanese will be besieged for seven years. Then the very
great leader [Napoleon] will make his entry there. The city will then be
freed from its enemies.

History

'The republics of both Venice and Genoa, where the patriciate was closely
identified with the State, but where too the resistance towards Austria
[the enemy, for the Italians] and the King of Sardinia was considerable,
seemed, despite their neutrality, to incline towards France.

Such were the dispositions of the Peninsula when the Emperor Francis
declared war *in 1792* upon the French Revolution, thus throwing Italy
into the struggle. . . . As soon as the war began, the rulers of Italy might
well have concluded that they did not have only the French to contend
with. The Emperor Francis had fresh troops go down through the Alps
into the Po Valley to contain *the Milanese* and support Victor-Amadeus
II. . . .

In May *1800*, Mélas got ready to cross the Var to invade Provence;
there was no hope left for Masséna, besieged with the last French troops
in Genoa. Suddenly Bonaparte descended through the Great St Bernard
Pass, came under fire – guns, baggage and all – from the stronghold of
Bard, and occupied part of Piedmont. After a long and heroic resistance
Masséna had surrendered the city of Genoa to the Austrians on 4 June.
But *the First Consul had already been in Milan* for two days, and there
he proclaimed the Republic anew, amid joy bordering on delirium. Mélas
led his troops back to the Po as fast as he could, hoping that such
boldness would prove justified. But Bonaparte again assumed command
of his army and on the plains of Marengo that 10 June completed what
his crossing of the St Bernard had begun so well. The French re-entered
Genoa; *the Emperor Francis*, quite stunned, *asked for an armistice so that
peace could be discussed: and France once again became the arbiter of Italian
destiny [Cité puis libre hors de ses ennemis].*'[2]

¹ Insubres: tribe of Cisalpine Gaul, who inhabited the northern Po region between the Adda, the Ticino and the Alps. Their main town was Mediolanum (Milan).DHB.
² HIJZ.

18 Brumaire. Bonaparte and His Two Brothers. The French Army on the Var

Aux fins¹ du Var changer le Pompotans,²
Près du rivage les trois beaux enfans³ naistre:
Ruyne au peuple par aage competans⁴
Regne au pays changer plus voir croistre.

CVIII,Q97

Interpretation

It is on the borders of the Var that the all-powerful aspects of England shall be changed. The career of three persons, as yet speechless, is to be born. After the ruin of the people which the [revolutionary] era had allowed, power shall know changes and grow still more.

History

'Fame and credit are due to Masséna, who had just executed one of the most perfect operations in the history of war, and who had saved us at a moment more dangerous than those of Valmy and Fleurus. . . . Zurich was the finest feather in Masséna's cap. . . .

While such fortunate events were going on in Switzerland, victory was ours once again in Holland. Brune had been only weakly pressed by the enemy and had time to concentrate his forces. *After defeating the British and the Russians* at Kastrikum, he had cornered them at the Zip and *forced them to surrender. . . .*

France was saved, but that was all; she had in no sense recovered her former standing, and still had dangers to contend with on the *Var*.

In the meanwhile Napoleon was quite calmly sailing the seas, which were *full of English ships*. Fearing after the recent events that the south of France might be invaded, he made not for *the coast of Provence but for that of the Languedoc*. He wanted to land at Collioure or Port-Vendres. Strong winds drove him towards Corsica. After that he sailed towards Toulon. Just as he was arriving, at dusk, thirty enemy ships were sighted to port, in the rays of the setting sun. It was suggested that a small boat should be lowered so they could land unobserved. Bonaparte, always a believer in destiny, said they would have to wait. Indeed, the enemy disappeared and on 17 Vendemiaire, Year VIII [8 October 1799], at daybreak, the frigates *Muiron* and *Carrère* and the xebecs *Revanche* and *Fortune* lay at anchor in the bay of Fréjus [*Près du rivage*]. . . .

His two brothers Lucien and Joseph [*trois beaux enfans*], along with his own deputies, *each day scored new victories* in the councils.

Such was the 18 Brumaire revolution, which was judged so differently: seen by some as the coup which destroyed our liberty, by others as a bold but necessary step *that ended anarchy* [*Ruyne au peuple*].'[5]

[1] For *confins*, borders, by aphesis.
[2] Used to denote England. Cf. cx,Q100, Vol. 1.
[3] *Infans:* one who does not talk, deprived of speech. D.LAT.
[4] *Si ejus competeret aetas:* if his age allowed him. Suetonius. D. LAT.
[5] HDEAT.

Napoleon Emperor Thanks to His Victories. Louis XVII Welcomed by the Vatican. Coalitions against Napoleon

Dresser copies[1] pour monter à l'Empire
Du Vatican le sang Royal tiendra:[2]
Flamens, Anglois, Espagne avec Aspire[3]
Contre l'Italie et France contendra.[4]

CVI,QI2

Interpretation

He [Bonaparte] will raise troops to ascend to the Empire. Royal blood will remain at the Vatican. The Flemish, the English, the Spanish united with the Germans will fight against Italy and France.

History

'The Directorate, driven by necessity, wanted an all-out simultaneous offensive. War must nurture war. *Italy* had to be conquered so as to be exploited. . . . On Bonaparte's arrival, the Italian Army was 35,000 strong. . . . The Directorate decided to dispatch 40,000 more men as reinforcements. . . .'

'Waterloo: England, Prussia, Austria and Russia each strove to keep

50,000 men in the field. An army made up of *Englishmen, Dutch* and *Germans* was united under Wellington in *Belgium.*'

'Although eleven months of effort and success had seen him almost back at his starting point, the year 1812 was not a fruitless one for Wellington. . . . The British general returned to Cadiz and had himself named C-in-C of *the Spanish troops.* The French evacuated Valladolid, then Burgos, and withdrew beyond the Ebro. Under a merciless sun the Spanish, Portuguese and British troops pursued them. . . .'

'By the peace treaty of 30 May 1814, France had abandoned all the conquests of the Revolution and the Empire; *Italy,* to which Napoleonic domination had at least bestowed an appearance of unity in its northern half, together with a government and national flag, was once again partitioned into ancient kingdoms and fell under the unwelcome hegemony of Austria. . . .'[5]

[1] Latin *copiae:* army corps, troops, military forces. D.LAT.
[2] Louis XVII would have been protected by the Vatican after his escape from the Temple Prison. Cf. CVI,Q51; CII,Q58; CIX,Q24 all Vol. I.
[3] For French Spire (by prothesis); English Speyer. Town in the Rhineland on a minor river of the same name. DHB.
[4] Latin *contendere:* to fight, struggle against. D.LAT.
[5] NEE.

Louis XVI, Madame Elizabeth, Louis XVII and His Sister in the Temple. The False Dauphins and the Bourbon Characteristics

Frères et soeurs en divers lieux captifs,
Se trouveront passer près du monarque:
Les contempler ses rameaux ententifs,[1]
Displaisant voir menton, front, nez, les marques.

CII,Q20

Interpretation

Brothers and sisters will be imprisoned in various areas [of the Temple]. They will be seen passing close to the king. People wishing to be descendants will be observed. Signs will be seen on the chin, forehead and nose of a disagreeable person [Naundorff].

History

'When they arrived at the Temple the illustrious captives were at first held in the part of the building called the Palace. . . . *Louis XVI slept on the second floor.* The Queen and *Madame Royale occupied a room on the first floor; the Dauphin,* his governess Madame de Tourzel, and the prince's chambermaid *were all lodged in one room adjoining;* the Princess de Lamballe was installed in a kind of antechamber. *Facing the King's room was another* which would serve as kitchen, and where the utensils were kept: *this was the accommodation for Madame Elizabeth* and Mlle de Tourzel [*En divers lieux*].'[2]

Brothers and sisters: on the one hand Louis XVI and his sister Madame Elizabeth, on the other, Louis XVII and his sister Madame Royale.

'What was more, according to expert opinion, Naundorff was nothing like the Bourbon type. Thus Louis Journot, invited by Senator Delahaye to compare portraits of Louis XVII and those of Naundorff [*contempler*], unhesitatingly remarked upon the two different types.'[3] In all the portraits Louis XVII has a straight *brow and nose,* while Naundorff has a bulging *forehead,* his *nose* prominently hooked. 'Once again then, Dr Galippe declared that none of the *descendants* [*rameaux*] showed the typical Hapsburg profile, that hereditary perculiarity which, even though absent in Naundorff, should have manifested itself among them.'[3]

[1] *Attentif:* intent, intention, end for which one aims. DAFI.
[2] *Historical Memoirs on Louis XVII,* M. Eckard, Paris, 1817.
[3] *Louis XVII, Critical Studies,* J.de Lathuy, Gembloux, 1976.

Napoleon's Military Coup against the Quirinal, 6 July 1809. Rebellion in Rome and the Campagna. Failure of Conscription

Dans temple[1] clos le foudre[2] y entrera,
Des Sitadins dedans leur fort[3] grevez[4]
Cheveaux, boeufs, hommes, londe,[5] mur[6] touchera,
Par faim soif, soubs les plus foibles armez.

CIII,Q6

Interpretation

Napoleon's army will enter the palace of the Catholic Church which had been closed. The town's inhabitants will be oppressed and in anguish. The men who deal with horses and cattle [peasants] will revolt as far as Rome, where hunger and thirst will be experienced, with very few conscripts.

History

'The Pope had Cardinal Pacca installed in his own apartment and put the Quirinal in a state of defensive readiness; thereafter entry was only to be effected *by breaking the doors in*. . . . General Miollis had to put the town *under martial law [grevés]* so as to prevent serious disorder. . . . The Pope was abducted on 6 July 1809 from his palace, whose doors were staved in by the leader of the Guard, Radet. . . .

A more general and perhaps more regrettable *opposition* came from the poor who had been *reduced to abject misery* by the banning of pilgrimages and the dispersion of the clergy – whose alms had kept these paupers idle while they rescued them from *starvation*. The population of *beggars*, 30,000 strong in Rome in 1812, numbered over 12,000 by the end of 1810, and begged even in front of the prefect's door. Rome in those days had a population of less than 140,000. . . .

The atmosphere changed completely when the Imperial administration sought to apply conscription to the towns and *countryside* surrounding the Papal State. . . . The percentage of conscripts reporting for call-up, out of all those actually conscripted, was *very low:* only 24 out of 300 showed up at Marino! In Umbria, the prefect of Trasimene was proud of having raised 140, but between Perugia and Florence they nearly all deserted. . . . Mass executions took place in Rome as well as in the Campagna.'[7]

[1] Poetic, for the Catholic Church. DLV.
[2] Cf. CI,Q65; CIII,Q44; and in Vol. I CII,Q76; CIII,Q13; CIV,Q43; CIV,Q54.
[3] Beset, in an anxious state. DAFL.
[4] To overwhelm, torment, oppress, tyrannize. DAFL.
[5] Nostradamus uses this word *passim* to denote revolt or rebellion.
[6] Cf. CIII,Q37, Vol. I.
[7] NEE.

The Beresina, November 1812. The Grand Army between the Dniepr and the Dwina

Entre deux fleuves se verra enserré,
Tonneaux et caques[1] unis à passer outre:
Huict pont rompus chef à tant enferré,[2]
Enfans parfaicts[3] sont jugulez[4] en coultre.[5]

CVIII,Q55

Interpretation

He [Napoleon] will see himself squeezed between two rivers [Dniepr and Dwina]. Barrels and casks of powder will have been bound together in order to cross to the other side; eight bridges will have been cut; the leader [Napoleon] will have fallen into a trap; children, having grown up, will be massacred.

History

'Among these stubborn marauders were many conscription-evaders and very few veterans. . . . Generally they were the *youngest*, the least unruly, the latter *taken from their families* by conscription [*enfans parfaicts*]. . . . The Young Guard, decimated by fighting and fatigue, still contained two thousand men.

Wittgenstein had taken up positions behind the Oula, which forms *the junction of the Dwina and Dniepr rivers*, beside the Lepel Canal and the Beresina. . . . In order to march on Moscow, Napoleon had gone through the open area *between* the Dniepr and the Dwina. Setting off, he had the Dwina on his left, the Dniepr on his right; on his return, the opposite was the case [*entre deux fleuves*].

It was not only *the bridges* over the racing waters which they found *cut*, but the bridges over the marshes, which were far longer and more difficult to cross. In contrast, by going along the Beresina towards its junction with the Oula, they discovered places where the river bed was shallow and sandy, and there they crossed with the waterline up to their belts [*enferré*].

The enemy, also exhausted, ceased firing round about midnight, sure of capturing every one of that handful of brave men who were stubbornly trying to get their *throats cut* [*jugulez en coultre*].[6]

---

[1] Barrel or cask for gunpowder or saltpetre. DL7V.
[2] To tie up, ensnare one's adversary, entrap him. DL7V.
[3] Latin *perfecta aetas*: legal age of majority, no longer a child. D.LAT.

4 Latin *jugulare:* to cut a throat, massacre, slaughter. D.LAT.
5 Latin *culter:* knife, either sacrificial or for butchery or hunting. D.LAT.
6 HDEAT.

Preparation for the Return from Elba, 1815. Napoleon and His Old Comrades-in-Arms

> Les Exilez par ire, haine intestine,
> Feront au Roy grand conjuration:
> Secret mettront ennemis par la mine,[1]
> Et ses vieux siens contre eux sédition.[2]

CI,QI3

Interpretation

The exiles, because of [the people's] anger and internecine hatred, will make a great conspiracy against the King. By secret machination they will mobilize against their enemies; and his former companions [Murat, Ney, etc.] will openly resist the King's authority.

History

'All the faults of Louis XVIII's administration were not lost upon the man *exiled* on the rocky Isle of Elba. . . . Bonaparte also watched with delight as papal anathema was directed against those who requisitioned national resources. From that moment he sought the next opportunity to overthrow the Bourbon dynasty [*Secret mettront ennemis par la mine*]. . . . All these acts – likely to alarm lovers of freedom – quickly bore fruit: the eastern departments showed themselves *hostile* to the government, while those in the Midi experienced outbursts of the most deplorable *feuds*. . . . Generals, officers and soldiers [*vieux siens*] all missed their tricolour cockades, their eagles, victories and, ultimately, their leader. . . .

Joachim Murat, learning that France was insisting that the crown of the Two Sicilies be restored to the lawful king of that country, declared his intention of crossing Italy in order to attack France. However absurd the idea of attacking France with 30,000 Neapolitans might have seemed, to Bourbon rule it was alarming, all the same. Napoleon counted on *his former comrades-in-arms* and on the irresistible power of public opinion. He did not toy with hatching a *conspiracy* – the first rumours of which

would inevitably have resulted in his being kept under the most embar-
rassing surveillance – but confiding his *secret* to none, he prepared to
carry out the boldest plan. Surrounded by eight or nine hundred soldiers
of his *Old Guard* and a few friends like Generals Bertrand, Drouot
and Cambrone, Napoleon anticipated the possibility of ending his *exile*,
crossing the Mediterranean and presenting himself to his *former*
companions in glory, with whom he hoped to overthrow the Bourbon
dynasty. . . . The very evening the Elba battalion was due to embark, a
carnival was held at Porto Ferrajo, and inhabitants as well as visitors
attended without suspecting its purpose as cover for the departure of
their celebrated host.'[3]

[1] *Mine secrète:* a secretive look, implying that one is hatching some kind of shady
plot. DL7V.
[2] Attack on or open resistance against established authority. DL7V.
[3] HFA.

Napoleon and the Return from Elba, 1 March 1815. The Treachery of Marie-Louise, September 1814

> Quand l'animal[1] à l'homme domestique,[2]
> Après grands peines et sauts[3] viendra parler,
> De foudre[4] à vierge[5] sera si maléfique,
> De terre prinse[6] et suspendue en l'air.[7]
>
> CIII,Q44

Interpretation

When the animal [Napoleon] comes to address the officers of his guard,
after great difficulties and leaps forward, the young woman [Marie-
Louise] will be very wicked towards the lightning [Napoleon], after he
has disembarked [from Elba], ready to set out.

History

'Napoleon was eager to give himself all the trappings of power. Ministers
. . . a court . . . above all, an army and a navy. To the 400 men of
the *Old Guard* were added 200 volunteers. . . . Since January 1815,
suggestions casually mooted showed that the idea [of returning] exercised
his mind [*suspendue en l'air*].

The audacity and resolution of Marshal Ney were being counted upon most of all. . . . "I'll deal with Bonaparte," Ney bellowed. "We'll attack that *beast!*"

Marie-Louise's treachery: instead of going to Italy, Marie-Louise returned to Vienna, where precautions had been taken to keep her son. . . . Since 8 September she had written that she would never go to Elba and would place in Metternich's hands all letters she might receive from Napoleon. Meanwhile, the *unfortunate* betrayed husband still deluded himself, and had apartments for his wife prepared. But her silence, along with bits of information garnered here and there, gradually enlightened him. His bitterness welled up in moving complaints: "My wife no longer writes to me. My son has been taken from me, as children of the vanquished once were, in order to deck the victors' triumph. In modern times one cannot think of such a *barbarity! [maléfique].*" [8]

[1] Beast is the term for an animal entirely devoid of intelligence. Animal, however, only applies *to creatures of a certain magnitude.* DL7V.

[2] Historical term, which after the fourth or fifth century AD referred to a body of soldiers of the *imperial guard*, and from the sixth applied specifically to officers. DL7V.

[3] Latin *saltus:* jump or rush forward. D.LAT.

[4] Cf. CI,Q65; CIII, Q6; and in Vol. I CII, Q76; CIII, Q13; CIV, Q43; CIV, Q54.

[5] Latin *virgo:* young woman. D.LAT. Marie-Louise, born 1791, was twenty-three in 1814.

[6] To land, disembark, reach land. DL7V.

[7] To be always in the air, i.e. ready to leave, run, jump. DL7V.

[8] NEE.

The Battle of Navarino, October 1827. Greek Independence, February 1830

Nautique rame invitera[1] les umbres,[2]
Du grand Empire[3] lors viendra conciter:[4]
La mer Aegée des lignes[5] desencombres,
Empeschant l'onde Thirrene[6] defflotez.

CV,Q95

Interpretation

A maritime power [nineteenth-century England] will challenge those who are no more than the shadows of their former selves [the Ottoman Empire in decline]. The great [British] Empire will mobilize its fleet to free the

Aegean Sea of [Turkish] battleships which were preventing navigation on the sea that bathes Thyrea [the Aegean].

History

'The death of Alexander 1 and his replacement by Nicholas 1 [December 1825], a believer in the strong approach, caused concern in *England*. In March 1826 Nicholas issued the Porte with an ultimatum whose consequence was the Treaty of Akerman: by it Russia secured the right to trade on all Ottoman Empire waters; *Greece* was not involved. *England*, unhappy with this Treaty, therefore *intervened*, and the London agreements anticipated the mediation of the three major powers [England, France and Russia] between Turkey and Greece. The Sultan rejected the offer of mediation and the Allies threatened him with armed intervention; *their fleet engaged* the Turkish and Egyptian fleets at Navarino where the latter were destroyed [October 1827]. . . . Finally the London Protocols [November 1828 and March 1829] established Greek borders, but it was the Russian Army which was entrusted with getting the new State recognized. . . . In February 1830, at the *London Conference*, Greece's independence was proclaimed. . . . Russian subjects were granted freedom of trade throughout all territories of the Ottoman Empire; at last the Bosphorus and Dardanelles Straits were *open to all merchant shipping* [desencombres].[7]

[1] Latin *invitare:* to provoke, challenge, engage. D.LAT.
[2] Symbolic, for person or thing whose brightness is diminished. DL7V.
[3] England. Cf. CX, Q100, Vol. 1.
[4] Latin *naves concitare:* to set sail. D.LAT.
[5] Nautical term for battle formation or ships at anchor. DL7V.
[6] Thyrea: town in Morea, in the Peloponnese, on the borders of Argolis and Laconia, near the Aegean coast. DHB. Example of paragoge.
[7] HDTRM.

The War of Greek Independence, 1821–28. Chios, Tripolis, Navarino, Trebizond

Au Chalmé[1] Duc, en arrachant[2] l'esponce,[3]
Voile Arabesque voir, subit descouverte:[4]
Tripolis[5] Chio,[6] et ceux de Trapesonce,[7]
Duc prins: Marnegro[8] et la cité déserte.

CVI, Q55

Interpretation

Because of General Maison's refusal to abandon [the Greeks] the Ottoman fleet will be spotted and exposed to enemy fire [Navarino]. After the massacres of Tripolis and Chios, with the aid of those [who will march on] Trebizond [the Russians], the commander-in-chief [Ibrahim] having surrendered, the Black Sea shall be liberated, the town [Tripolis] laid waste.

History

'The Morea expedition had just been decided upon. General *Maison* won the command from all his rivals. He was entrusted with the dubious honour of pursuing Ibrahim and stopping that ferocious *Arab's* depredations in Greece.'[9]

'In 1824 Ibrahim assumed command of the Egyptian Army sent to fight the Greeks. Attacked at sea by Admiral Miaoulis, he lost half his force but landed at Modos [February 1825] and took Navarino, Tripolitza, Argos and Missolonghi. Blockaded after the sea battle of Navarino, Ibrahim Pasha, on his father's orders, signed an honourable *surrender*. [*Duc prins*].'[10]

'In the Morea, Germanos, Archbishop of Patras, declared a War of Liberation [25 March 1821]. . . . In April the notorious massacres at *Chios* took place and in May Joannina fell to the Turks. . . . On 20 December 1827 the Sultan proclaimed a Holy War, which gave the Russians a pretext to declare war on him in April 1828. . . . French military intervention in the Morea was effected without difficulty, an agreement being signed with Mehmet Ali (November 1828). Finally the London Protocols (November 1828 and March 1829) fixed the borders of Greece, but the Russian Army took on the task of enforcing recognition of the new State: attacking in the east, it seized Erzerum and advanced upon Trebizond. . . . Freedom of trade was granted to Russian subjects throughout the entire Ottoman Empire, and at last the Bosphorus and Dardanelles Straits [*Marnegro*] were open to all merchant shipping.'[11]

'*Tripolitza,* prosperous capital of the *Morea* under the Turks, was captured and recaptured during the War of Independence, notably by Mehmet Ali (1825), and almost *razed [et la cité déserte].*'[12]

¹ From *chalme* or *chaume.* DAFL. Hence *chaumière,* small thatched *house* or cottage. DL7V. An astonishing codification of General Maison's name.
² Figurative: to banish or deprive of. DL7V.
³ *Esponce:* archaic word meaning scattering or abandonment. DL7V.
⁴ To expose oneself to an enemy's or opponent's blows. DL7V.
⁵ Tripolitza, *Tripolis.* Greek town, almost in the centre of the *Morea.* DHB.
⁶ Greek island near the Turkish coast: Chios is its chief town. DHB.
⁷ Trebizond, Trapezus, town and port in Asia Minor on the *Black Sea.* DHB. The -us ending has been changed for the sake of the rhyme with *esponce.*
⁸ Neologism from two Latin words, *mare* and *niger,* the Black Sea.
⁹ HFA.
¹⁰ DL7V.
¹¹ HDTRM.
¹² DHB.

War in Piedmont. Mortara, March 1849. Defeat of Mortara before that of Novara.

Le tremblement de terre à Mortara,[1]
Cassich[2] sainct George[3] a demy perfondrez:[4]
Paix assoupie, la guerre esveillera.
Dans temple[5] à Pasques abysmes[6] enfondrez.[7]

CIX,Q31

Interpretation

War will shake the earth at Mortara. Because of a trap, half the Italian Army will be overthrown. Peace being weary, war shall break out again. In the Catholic Church, at Easter, there will be disaster.

History

'On 5 March, after the Turin Parliament and the Council of Lombard refugees *had formally called for war,* the King accepted Gioberti's resignation, and took on a new government comprised of *the pro-war majority,* with Ratazzi as President. On the twelfth, and this despite French and English representations, the King denounced the armistice to General Radetzky. . . . Hostilities began on the twentieth. The same day, rioting

broke out at Brescia. Crzanowski's intention was to force the Austrians
back on the Naviglio Grande so he could press on to Milan; Ramorino,
on the right flank, and sent to *Mortara*, had the job of keeping watch on
the enemy at Pavia and of aiding La Marmora. But during the night of
the nineteenth Radetzky had withdrawn his troops to Pavia, and for his
part had thrown a bridge across the Lower Ticino, over which two of
his brigades had crossed to the right bank, encountering no resistance
from Ramorino, who remained inactive. This grave error proved
decisive. On the twenty-first the Piedmontese Army recrossed the Ticino
to confront the Austrians, who were continuing to emerge from Pavia.
Durando was sent in the vanguard to reinforce *Mortara*. Crzanowski led
the rest to Sforzesca and Vigevano in order to support him. But delay in
the arrival of supplies halted several brigades. The Piedmontese resisted
brilliantly at Sforzesca on the twenty-first, without being able to check
the Austrian advance, and Durando, almost cut off at *Mortara*, allowed
this village to be captured in a night attack *at a cost of two thousand
men killed or taken prisoner* . . . The defeat at Novara led to the fall of
Brescia. . . .

Mazzini, who had been in Rome since 6 March, became a member of
the Triumvirate on the twenty-ninth, the day on which news of the
defeat at Novara reached Rome. A new Rienzi, who combined a tribune's
passion with a mystic's fervour, he believed he could save the situation
by invoking, in that eternal city, God and the people, *on the ruins* of the
government and *of the Church*.'[8]

[1] Town in Italy (Piedmont), 23 km south-south-east of Novara. DHB.
[2] Traps, ambushes. D.LAT.
[3] Company of St George, regiment of *condottieri*. 'He had taken on to his payroll the
Company of St George, a wholly Italian group. . . .' HIJZ.
[4] Latin *perfundere:* to disrupt, disturb. D.LAT.
[5] Poetic allusion to Roman Catholic Church. DL7V.
[6] Fig.: dangers or perils. DL7V.
[7] Latin *infundere:* to penetrate, introduce into. D.LAT.
[8] HIJZ.

Garibaldi from Sicily and Naples to Rome, 1860–67. The Agreement between Garibaldi and the British. The Shortcomings of Francis II, King of the Two Sicilies

Le mouvement des sens, coeur, pieds et mains,
Seront d'accord Naples, Lyon, Sicille.[1]
Glaives,[2] feux, eaux puis aux nobles Romains,
Plongez, tuez, morts par cerveau debile.

CI,QII

Interpretation

Through the progress of ideas, by a common feeling, feet and hands united, they shall be in accord with the British Lion for the expedition against Naples and Sicily. The battles, fires and revolutionary upheavals will win over the noble Romans [clergy]; the revolutionaries having been killed and put to death by one of feeble mind [Francis 11].

History

'Francis II, aged twenty-three, a dreary and simple character [*cerveau débile*] had succeeded Ferdinand upon the latter's death in 1859. . . . Dominated by a gerontocracy, the royal family of *Naples* was also wracked by sinister intrigues which weakened it day by day. Crispi reported to Garibaldi that *the revolution* had been *bloodily suppressed* [*plongez, tuez, morts*] at Palermo [Sicily], but that it continued nonetheless to *spread* [*mouvement des sens*] in the country areas. . . . After the Palermo setback the Bourbon troops in Sicily were augmented to about five thousand soldiers, based at Messina. The rest of the island came under the control of the new dictatorial government. The London *Times* hailed Garibaldi's triumph in the headline: "He Succeeds!" . . . At that time Garibaldi was the only foreigner to arouse such enthusiasm in *England* [*Lyon*], with his Sicilian expedition [*accord . . . Lyon, Sicille*]. . . . After the seizure of Palermo it became necessary to extend the war to the mainland, with Naples as objective. . . . The expedition against *Rome*, in autumn 1867, was one of the saddest episodes in Garibaldi's life. There he experienced one of the rare military defeats of his career, all the more bitter because it was inflicted by the French and the Pope. . . . Garibaldi succeeded in scoring an initial success by routing the papal forces and occupying Monterotondo. . . . The battle took place at Mentana. The enemy was numerically superior, with nine thousand papal troops [*nobles Romains*] and two thousand Frenchmen against five thousand on Garibaldi's side. . . .'[3]

¹ The Kingdom of the Two Sicilies consisted of two distinct parts: the Kingdom of
Naples, and Sicily itself. . . . Francis II was expelled from Naples in 1860. His
departure saw the end of the Kingdom of the Two Sicilies, which was annexed in 1861
and became part of the Kingdom of Italy. DHB.
² Symbol of war and battles. DL7V.
³ GP and MR.

End of the Pope's Temporal Power, 1870. Role of the Secret Societies. Internal Struggles

> Romain pouvoir sera du tout à bas,
> Son grand voisin imiter les vestiges:¹
> Occultes haines civiles et debats,
> Retarderont aux boufons leur folies.

CIII,Q63

Interpretation

[The Pope's temporal] Power shall be laid low in Rome, following in the
footsteps of his great neighbour [France]. The hatred of the secret societies, in civil wars and disputes, will delay the follies of these clowns.

History

'There remained to Pius IX Rome, Civitavecchia and a few small
fortresses manned by French garrisons. An attack by Garibaldi in 1867
was repulsed at Mentana by papal troops supported by French forces.
But after the disasters of 1870 the French left *Rome* and the King of
Italy's army entered the city after a brief skirmish on 20 September, the
day *the Pope's temporal power*, constituted by Pepin the Short and by
Charlemagne, *came to an end*. Rome became the capital of the Kingdom
of Italy.'²

'The vote on the civil constitution of the clergy in July 1790 had graver
consequences. This constitution had been drawn up by the Gallican
Catholics who were *opposed to Papal supremacy*. The Pope did not even
officiate at the spiritual investiture: he was merely informed of the
election.'³

'In Italy, the pioneers of the revolution called themselves "Carbonari".
The Carbonari were *a secret society* [*occultes haines*] which preached assassination as a political weapon and whose ultimate aim was the destruction

of authoritarian regimes and the creation of egalitarian republics. One of its leaders was Filippa Buonaroti, an Italian aristocrat and naturalized Frenchman, *a friend of Robespierre* and precursor of revolutionary socialism. . . . A first insurrection fermented by Sardinian and Neapolitan officers *affiliated to* the Carbonari erupted simultaneously at Turin and Naples in 1821. . . . Nine years later, the *French Revolution of July 1830 had repercussions in Italy.* Modena and Bologna were the centres of rebellions which Metternich brutally suppressed. . . . In 1833, *Garibaldi made an important discovery as regards his political thinking: he became familiar with St-Simon's form of socialism.* Count St-Simon, an aristocrat who had miraculously escaped the guillotine during the Terror, wrote works in which he outlined a plan for the equal distribution of wealth and common ownership of property.'[4]

[1] Latin *vestigium:* trace. D.LAT.
[2] DHB.
[3] HFAM.
[4] GP and MR.

Garibaldi in Brazil, 1835. The Hohenzollern Candidacy to the Spanish Throne. The Duke of Aosta as King of Spain, 1870. Garibaldi's Landing at Marseille, 1870. The Advent of the Third Republic

Siècle nouveau,[1] alliance nouvelle,
Un Marquisat[2] mis dedans la nacelle,[3]
A qui plus fort des deux l'emportera;
D'un Duc[4] d'un Roy, gallere de Florence,[5]
Port à Marseille, Pucelle dans la France,
De Catherine fort chef on rasera.

Sixain 1

Interpretation

In a century of revival [the nineteenth], new alliances will take place. The head of a marquisate will be chosen for Spain. Will the Duke [of Aosta] or the King [William] be successful? A ship shall take [to Spain] [the heir] of Florence. [Garibaldi] shall land at Marseille to assist the return of the Republic to France; he who will have been present at the devastation of [Santa] Catarina.

History

'In September 1835, the eight thousand kilometres separating *Marseille* from Rio were travelled in eighty days. This richly adventurous period established him as a legendary fighter for freedom and national liberation. . . .'

The inhabitants of Santa Catarina soon lost their illusions after welcoming Gonzalves and his men as liberators. When several towns rebelled against the tyranny of the gauchos, Gonzalves decided to punish them for their disobedience and ordered Garibaldi to administer a stern lesson to one of their number, Imahury. The *repression was viciously cruel* and its memory was to haunt Garibaldi to the end of his days. The republicans were let loose to wreak savage havoc, *sacking and burning* houses and shops, massacring children and old people and raping women.'[6]

'On 15 July 1870, Benedetti met *King* William in the Park at Ems. He asked the latter for permission to announce that he would forbid Prince Hohenzollern to renew his candidature [for the Spanish throne].'[7]

'*Who would be king? Spain* entrusted her ambassadors with interviewing all the available princes of Europe. There were numerous refusals, but some acceptances, among them that of Leopold of Hohenzollern. Discussions between France, opposed to the rule of a Prussian in Spain, and Bismarck, led to the famous Ems Telegram which started the Franco-Prussian War of 1870. Finally, Amedeo of Savoy, Duke of Aosta, son of Victor Emmanuel II, declared his willingness to assume the throne of Spain. . . . The new sovereign arrived in Madrid on 2 January 1871.'[8]

'The Italian government was hardly concerned at seeing the dangerous agitator [Garibaldi] leave to work miracles in France. The war with the Prussians represented a good way of getting rid of him, and many of Victor Emmanuel II's entourage must have hoped he would not return. At Bonifacio Garibaldi found a yacht – the *Ville de Paris* – lent by a wealthy Marseille businessman of republican and progressive views. At *Marseille* he received a triumphant welcome. Delighted and moved at his reception by the people of Marseille, Garibaldi wrote to a friend: "To my dying day I shall be proud *to serve the sacred cause of the Republic.*" '

---

[1] The nineteenth century saw changes not only of rule but also of institutions and laws (*Code Civil* in France). All the alliances of the Ancien Régime would be revised.

[2] The Marches were called *marchiones*, later Margraves or *Marquises*. In Charlemagne's time the marches were composed of the Saxon March and the Friulian March in Italy . . . DL7V. Thus the use of the word marquisate for the Val d'Aosta.

[3] Denotes Spain. Cf. CV,Q49.

⁴ Amedeo I abdicated on 10 February 1873. He returned to Italy, took up his previous title of Duke of Aosta, and received his former emolument. DL7V.

⁵ Amedeo I was the son of Victor Emmanuel II, King of Italy, whose capital was *Florence*. Cf. CV,Q39, Vol. I.

⁶ GP and MR.

⁷ LSEOA.

⁸ HDEJP.

The Succession to the Spanish Throne a Cause of the Franco-Prussian War of 1870. French Troops Surrounded at Metz. The Eastern Army at Villersexel.

Tous ceux de Illerde[1] seront dans la Moselle,
Mettant à mort tous ceux de Loire et Seine,
Le cours[2] marin viendra près d'Hautevelle,[3]
Quand Espagnols ouvrira toute veine.

CI,Q89

Interpretation

Germans and Austrians will enter the Moselle area, decimating the armies of the Loire and Paris. He who will have come by sea shall approach Hautevelle. When the Spaniards leave open the succession to the throne [good fortune for the Hohenzollerns].

History

'Owing to a revolution, *the Spanish throne had been vacant* since 1868. *The Spaniards were seeking a king.* Suddenly, on 2 July 1870, Prince Leopold of Hohenzollern, cousin of the King of Prussia, announced his candidacy. Public opinion in France fell into the trap and all common sense was instantly abandoned. It seemed obvious to everyone that a Prussian Prince ruling Spain meant that France would be caught between two fires, and there was talk of the return of the Empire of Charles V. . . .'

'Following the agreements of 1866, men from Baden and *Württemberg*, as well as *Bavarians*, marched alongside the Prussians. . . . There were three French armies in the field that December and January: the Northern Army under Faidherbe, the 2nd *Loire* Army under Chanzy, and the Eastern Army under Bourbaki.'[4]

'According to Moltke's plan, the Germans regrouped into three armies. The first, on the right flank, marched along *the Moselle*. . . . Facing the Crown Prince was MacMahon, who had *hastened from Algeria* [*cours marin*] and now had to defend Alsace. . . .'[5]

'Victor of *Villersexel* [9 January 1871], Bourbaki could not break the lines at Héricourt. Pushed back upon Besançon, then to the Swiss frontier, and caught between two German armies, the Eastern Army only escaped surrender by rushing into Switzerland, where it was disarmed.'

'However, to hasten the capitulation of Paris [*Seine*] the Germans began the bombardment of the town. . . . A sortie was attempted by ninety thousand men on 19 January, pushing towards Buzenval and Montretout on the plateaux overlooking the Seine, west of Paris. This proved a new and *bloody* failure.'[6]

[1] The Iller, German river, whose source is in the north-west Tyrol, separates *Bavaria from Württemberg,* and meets the Danube 2 km above Ulm. DHB. Nostradamus denotes, by naming this river, both Germans and Austrians. Example of paragoge.
[2] Fig.: march, progress. DL7V.
[3] Commune of the Haute-Saône, 15 km from Villersexel.
[4] HFAM.
[5] LSEOA.
[6] HFAM.

1830–70: Forty Years of War.
1871–1914: Forty Years of Peace

Par quarante ans l'Iris[1] n'apparoistra,
Par quarante ans tous les jours sera veu:
La terre aride[2] en siccité[3] croistra,
En grand déluges[4] quand sera aperceu.

CI,QI7

Interpretation

For forty years peace will not be known, then for forty years there will be peace every day. The minds of men will become arid and dry when great revolutions are seen [1917].

History

1830: Departure from Toulon of the French fleet, sent to Algiers.

1831: French expedition in Portugal.

1832: Occupation of Ancona by the French. Siege of Anvers and capture of that town.

1833: Naval battle at Cape St Vincent.

1834: The French repel six thousand Kabyles invading from Bejaia in Algeria.

1835: Expedition against Mascara.

1836: Tlemcen and Constantine expeditions.

1837: Constantine captured.

1838: French intervention at La Plata: capture by the French of Martin-Garcia Island (Argentina). French intervention in Mexico.

1839: French actions at Portes-de-Fer, Algeria.

1840: Heroic defence by the garrison of Fort Mazagran. Occupation of Cherchell, Medeah, Milianah. Bombardment of Beirut and fall of Sidon, Lebanon.

1841: Seizure by the French of the Nossi-Bé and Nossi-Komba islands in the Indian Ocean.

1842: Occupation of Mayotte and the islands of Tahiti and the Marquesas.

1843: Duke of Aumale captures the Smala of Abd-el-Kader. Occupation of Assinia, Grand-Bassam, and Gabon.

1844: Capture of Oujda. Bombardment of Tangier and Mogador. Campaign against the Kabyles.

1845: Anglo-French expedition against Tamatava. Kabyle uprising. Anglo-French fleet goes into battle against the dictator Rosas, at Obligado, in support of Uruguayan independence.

1846: Abd-el-Kader leaves the desert, swoops upon the Titteri territory and appears among the Kabyles of the Dellys circle; the Emir is pursued into Moroccan territory by General Cavaignac.

187: In Algeria, the surrender of the agitator Boumaza. Cochin China expedition. Failure of Anglo-French operations against the Hovas on Madagascar. Surrender of Abd-el-Kader.

1848: Revolution and fierce fighting in Paris. State of siege declared.

*1849:*French expeditionary force sent to Italy to aid the King of Piedmont. Siege and occupation of Rome (2 and 3 July). In Algeria, rebellions against the French are suppressed.

1850: Riots in Algeria. Arrests at Lyon and Avignon over a conspiracy involving several departments in the Midi.

1851: Bombardment of Rabat and Sale by Rear-Admiral Dubourdieu.

1852: Surrender by ninety-two delegates from seventeen different branches of the Zaouaouas, in Greater Kabylia. The Sherif of Ourgla is forced into Laghonat, which falls to General Pelissier.

1853: Occupation of New Caledonia. Generals Bousquet and MacMahon defeat the Kabyles of the Babor Mountains between Setif, Bejaia and Djidjelli.

1854: Landings in the Crimea. Victory of the Alma. Siege of Sebastopol.

1855: Military advances as far as the oases of Ouargla and Metlili. Operations in the Djurjura – capture of Touggourt. Capture of Sebastopol in the Crimea.

1856: Expeditions by the Renault and Yusuf divisions against the Kabyles.

1857: Generals Renault and Yusuf force the Kabyle surrender. War with the Moors on the left bank of the Senegal River.

1858: After three years of war, treaty with the King of the Trarzas in Senegal.

1859: War in Italy – battles of Magenta and Solferino.

1860: French expedition into Syria against the Druzes. China expedition. Capture of Peking.

1861–62: War in Cochin China. Treaty of Hué. The French from Rome occupy Terracina.

1863: Mexico: expeditionary force sets out from Orizaba against Puebla – occupation of Queretaro. War in Cochin China against Tu-Duc.

1864: Riots in various Algerian towns. Struggle of the Franco-Chinese army against the Taipings.

1865: An uprising of the Babor tribes in Algeria is suppressed. Pinet campaign. Laprade in Gambia. Mexican War.

1866: Mexican War. Insurrections at Sidon and Géryville. Expedition in Cochin China against the Cambodians. Fighting against the cannibals in New Caledonia.

1867: End of war in Mexico. In Senegal, struggle against Maba partisans. Fighting in Cochin China. Intervention against Garibaldi in Italy.

1868: Rebellion in western Algeria after the death of Si-Hamza. Demonstration of St Denis, Réunion Island, bloodily suppressed. French outpost surprised by force of Annamites.

1869: Rebellion of the Ouled-Sidi-Sheik in Algeria. In Senegal, expedition against a fanatical chieftain, Ahmadou Sekhou, and against Lat-Dior.

1870: Franco-Prussian War.

Forty years of war on an extraordinary variety of different fronts!

1871–1913: Forty-two years of peace centred round the Belle Epoque.

¹ Iris, personification of the rainbow, regarded as the messenger of the gods. DCBM.
Rainbow: symbolizes all that is pleasant, alluding to the biblical meteor by which God
showed Noah that he would never again lose the earth by *flood*. DL7V.
    ² 'There came a time of *dryness* and lassitude, when *arid* speculations were indulged
in.' St-Evremont. DL.
    ³ Dryness (*sécheresse*).
    ⁴ By analogy, a considerable cataclysm with the earth its theatre. DL7V. Here
implying, as do the words *water* and *flood*, revolution.

The Russian Revolution Leads to Famine and Disaster, 1917. Human Rights Ignored. Battles of the Somme 1916–18

Si grand famine par unde¹ pestifère
Par pluye² longue le long du polle artique:
Samarobryn³ cent lieux de l'hemisphere
Vivront sans loy exempt de pollitique.⁴

CVI,Q5

Interpretation

A disastrous revolution will lead to a great famine. This revolution will
affect a hundred places in the Northern Hemisphere during the battles.
Men shall live without law in aid of the citizens.

History

'Revolution in Russia. In Switzerland in January 1917 Lenin said that
his generation would not live long enough to see the triumph of the
Revolution in Russia, and, in a single week, from 8 to 15 March, the
Romanov Empire was finished.'⁵
    'Ludendorff's offensives. Picardy, 21 March–5 April. The *Michel*
operation was intended to drive the British back to the sea and
surrounding the French left flank . . . The sequence of battle began with
the destruction of Gough's army south of the Somme, followed by a rapid
push for *Amiens*, whose outskirts were reached on the thirtieth. . . .'⁵
    'The Great Purge, by which he [Stalin] set himself up as undisputed
dictator, consisted of three basic elements: above all, the scale of the
operation created *millions of victims*, while each member of the population
felt threatened; then there were the methods adopted, in particular the

extraordinary ordeal of confession, during which the dictator's main opponents publicly accused themselves of treason; finally, there was the air of mystery surrounding it: the only exception to this was a number of show trials held in public and various announcements of executions. Otherwise, nothing of the Purge was officially admitted [*sans loy exempt de pollitique*].'[6]

'The economic revival was halted in 1922 by *the great famine* which ravaged the entire agricultural region of the Ukraine, and those of the Volga and Western Siberia.'[7]

[1] Latin *unda:* movement of a crowd, agitation, trouble. D.LAT.
[2] Rain, used in the same sense as above.
[3] Samarobriva, town in Gaul, capital of the Ambii. D.LAT. Now Amiens.
[4] Greek: Πολιτιϰός, relative or proper to citizens, civil, civic. DG.
[5] PANS.
[6] LGT.
[7] USDH.

The First World War Follows the Belle Epoque. Progress in Travel by Land, Sea and Air. Twentieth-century Wars

Les fleurs[1] passez, diminue le monde,[2]
Long temps la paix, terres inhabitées,
Sur marchera par ciel, terre, mer et onde,
Puis de nouveau les guerres suscitées.

CI,Q63

Interpretation

After the Belle Epoque, there shall be fewer people; after a long period of peace [1871–1914], lands shall no longer be inhabited. Men will know how to travel in the sky, by land, sea and under water. Then new wars will break out.

History

The First World War brought France brutally out of the Belle Epoque and plunged her into a nightmare. The battle zones, littered with shells and mines, were to remain uninhabited for some years afterwards.

The 1871–1914 period would see engineering developments and improvements change the face of man's travel: trains, motor cars, aeroplanes, steamships and submarines [*onde*].

Anarchist Movements in Spain, 1897–1939. Exile of Alfonso XIII, 1931. Franco and the Civil War Bloodbath, 1936–39

Lorsque serpens[1] viendront circuire[2] l'are,[3]
Le sang Troyen[4] vexé par les Espagnes:
Par eux grand nombre en sera faict tare,[5]
Chef fruict,[6] caché[7] au mares dans les saignes.

CI,QI9

Interpretation

When the Anarchists come and show themselves in the [Spanish] land, Bourbon blood will be troubled in the regions of Spain. A great number of deaths will be caused by these Anarchists. A leader [Franco] will benefit from this and drive them into pools of blood.

History

'Anarchism. The Spanish workers' demands are much the same as those of other European proletarian movements. What distinguishes Spain however is the *Anarchist* element, far more influential in the Iberian peninsula, where it became guerrilla ideology. Its ideal was direct action, *assassination.* . . .

Between 1897 and 1923 Anarchism had to its credit the assassinations of three heads of government, Canovas, Canalejas and Dato, not counting several unsuccessful attempts upon the life of the King of Spain. The Anarchists declared war on the Church, the Army and society. As regards the former, various churches in Barcelona had been burned down since the 'Tragic Week' of 1909, and this happened again at the start of the Civil War in 1936. As for the bourgeoisie, a bomb was thrown into the stalls of the Lyceum Theatre in Barcelona, and during a religious procession in the same town.'[8]

The Republic was proclaimed in 1931, when Alfonso XIII was forced into exile.

'In the Republican zone, persecution of the Church had begun in 1936 at the start [of the war]; numerous religious buildings were burned and sacked, and many priests shot or imprisoned. . . . In the Nationalist zone, anyone suspected of contacts with left-wing organizations became the target for persecution. Various executions were carried out also by unaffiliated groups. But the majority of the death sentences were pronounced by the military tribunals which functioned continuously throughout the conflict. . . . The number of those on both sides who died because of their political beliefs was very high. A rough estimate was 750,000 dead [pools of blood]. . . .'[8]

[1] Nostradamus here denotes revolutionary anarchists. Cf. C I I , Q 4 3 , Vol. I.
[2] To go the rounds of. DAFL.
[3] The entire surface. Used here to denote the whole country.
[4] Cf. CVI, Q52, Vol. I.
[5] *Tarer:* to spoil, corrupt. DL.
[6] Fig.: profit, advantage, useful result. DL7V.
[7] Latin *cogere:* to push in front of one, chase, force, drive violently. D.LAT.
[8] HEFDP.

The Russo-German Pact, 23 August 1939. The German Wheat Shortage, 1939

> La Sangsue[1] au loup[2] se joindra,
> Lorsqu'en mer le blé défaudra,
> Mais le grand Prince sans envie,
> Par ambassade luy donra
> De son blé pour lui donner vie,
> Pour un besoin s'en pourvoira.
>
> Sixain 7

Interpretation

The USSR will ally with Germany when the supplies of wheat by sea are lacking. But the great leader [Stalin] will gladly bring his aid through an embassy and will supply the wheat to alleviate want.

History

'The USSR is neutral should there be a German-Polish War. Even more curious and important is the recent approach by the Soviet *ambassador* in Warsaw, Mr Charonov, who was eager to convince Colonel Beck that the Soviet government had nothing but friendly intentions towards Poland.'

'In Germany at this very time the civilian population has been enlisting. . . . Starting today, *bread ration cards* are being introduced. To quote Dr Schacht: "One cannot end a war with bread rationing, nor can one begin a war with bread rationing." Does Herr Hitler distrust the warning given by the man who in the Third Reich has the reputation of being the most realistic of politicians?'[3]

[1] The leech, or blood-drinker, i.e. the revolutionary USSR. Cf. Sixains 21, 30, 40, and 46, Vol. 1.
[2] Cf. CV,Q4, Vol. 1.
[3] Extracts from an article by Jean Thouvenin in *L'Intransigeant*, 29 August 1939.

Mussolini and Clara Petacci Taken by Lorry to Milan. The Seven Corpses at Piazzale Loreto in Milan, 29 April 1945

> Serpens[1] transmis[2] en la cage de fer,
> Où les enfans[3] septains[4] du Roy sont prins:
> Les vieux et pères sortiront bas de l'enfer,
> Ains mourir voir de fruict mort et cris.

CI,QIO

Interpretation

The wicked one will be transported in a lorry to the place where the seven abominable persons of the [Fascist] Regime are guarded. The elderly and the relatives will leave their homes [in order to indulge in] mean acts. They will want to see the dead, amid cries and fruits [refuse].

History

'It was 8 p.m. when a large yellow *van* from Dongo reached Mezzagra with its macabre load. Clara was thrown on top of the heap first, followed by Mussolini. At 8.15 the van moved on towards Como and Milan.'

'Around 7 a.m. in the cold Sunday dawn of 29 April 1945, the first passers-by approached. The crowd swelled rapidly. The news spread that Mussolini's corpse was there! At 9 a.m. there was complete hysteria.

A woman came and fired five revolver shots into the Duce's body, *screaming* [*cris*] that she was thus avenging her five sons killed during the war. . . . It triggered off a chain reaction. The crowd soon became uncontrollable. Assorted scraps of *vegetables* were thrown at the bodies. People spat on them. . . . Anyone who wanted to do so "heroically" kicked Mussolini's body and Clara Petacci's too. One termagant urinated on the Duce's face. . . . A man stuck a stick into Mussolini's hand for a sceptre and a crown of *cabbage* leaves round his head [*bas de l'enfer*].

At 11 a.m. the corpses were strung up by ropes on the forecourt of a filling station: Mussolini, Clara, Pavolini, Zerbino, Barracu and Porta. The crowd *shrieked* with joy and insulted the *idol* [*serpent*] it had worshipped. Shortly afterwards, at 11.10 a.m., the former general secretary of the party, Achille Starace, was led there and six partisans shot him in the back. His body also was strung up alongside those hanging there [6+1=7]. The crowd was delirous until almost one o'clock, its collective *hysteria* indescribable.'[5]

[1] Symbolic of a perfidious, evil person. DL7V.
[2] Latin *transmitto:* I transport. D.LAT.
[3] Latin *infans:* abominable, frightful. D.LAT.
[4] Septain – group of seven similar things. DAFL.
[5] MAB.

Hesitation over the Provence Landing, August–December 1943. The German Occupation as far as Monaco. Imprisonment of Mussolini. Mussolini Hanged in Milan, 29 April 1945

> De sang et faim plus grand calamité,
> Sept fois[1] s'appreste à la marine plage:
> Monech de faim, lieu pris, captivité,
> Le grand mené croc[2] enferrée[3] cage.[4]

CIII,QIO

Interpretation

Through blood and famine the calamity will be still greater. Several times preparations will be made to land on the coast [of Provence]. Hunger will reach Monaco, this place having been occupied. After his captivity the great [Mussolini] shall be driven in a van and displayed from an iron hook.

History

'The operation codenamed Anvil had been called Dragoon since 1 August in order to throw German intelligence off the scent, and *this operation, which ought to have liberated the whole of the South of France in record time, had run into difficulties from the first.* Within Allied Command itself, as well as in its relationship with the French, different arguments had *cast doubt* upon the success and even the very *existence of the operation.*

First, the whole principle of the landing had been criticized, on political as well as military grounds.

While the Quebec Conference of August 1943, convened to decide on the creation of the second front, had suggested a southern landing to liaise with the Normandy one, and the December 1943 Teheran Conference had confirmed the plan, *the appropriateness of Operation Anvil was constantly being questioned* [*sept fois s'appreste*] as the date set for it drew ever nearer. . . .'[5]

'German Defences. The 19th Army had the task of defending the 650 km of coastline between *Menton* and Cerbère, and on *the day of the landing* six infantry divisions were regrouped along either bank of the Rhône.'[6]

'Between 1940 and 1944, *the principality was occupied* first by the Italians, then by the Germans, for military purposes.'[7]

'Mussolini's imprisonment at the de Marias': "As a temporary *prison*, it was ideal. . . . At 11 a.m. six of the corpses were strung up by ropes on *the forecourt* of the filling station: Mussolini, Clara, Pavolini, Zerbino, Barracu and Porta. . . ." '[8]

---

[1] In the Bible, the number 7 is often used to denote a considerable amount, as we might say 'hundreds'. DL7V.

[2] Another name for the hooks used to hang meat from. DL7V.

h5[3] Latin *inferre:* to present, display. D.LAT.

[4] Cf. CI,Q10; CII,Q24, in Vol. I, and CIX,Q95.

[5] HLFRA.

[6] LDG.

[7] From *History of Monaco* by J. B. Robert. PUF: *Que Sais-je*, No. 497.

[8] MAB.

The Link-up between the French, American, British and Russian Armies on the Danube, April–May 1945. Mussolini in a Van and the Fall of Hitler, 29 April 1945

Bestes farouches de faim fleuves tranner,[1]
Pluspart du champ encotre Hister[2] sera,
En cage de fer[3] le grand fera traisner,
Quand rien enfant[4] de Germain observera.

CII,Q24

Interpretation

They shall cross the rivers like wild and ravenous beasts. The larger part of the field [of battle] will be on the Danube. The great one [Mussolini] will be hauled in a van, when nothing more of the abominable German [Hitler] can be seen.[5]

History

'The Rhine-*Danube* Campaign. The fifth and final act of the "Rhine and *Danube*" campaign consisted of a pincer action by Monsabert and Béthouart, whose objective was Ulm [Ulm is on the Danube]; the former, with his 5th Armoured Division and 2nd Infantry Division (General de Linarès) north of the *Danube*, the latter thrusting his 1st Armoured Division (General Sudre) at the main Donaueschingen-Biberach road, *south of the river.* . . .'

'Liberation of *Vienna*. But already by 2 April, advancing between Lake Neusiedl and the *Danube*, Malinowski had forced the Mur at Bruck, while Tolbukin, in possession of the important industrial centre of Wiener Neustadt, pushed forward one column on to the Semmering road towards Graz and another on to Mödling and the Austrian capital. . . . Marshal Tolbukin, who was revelling in the capture of 130,000 prisoners, 1,350 tanks and 2,250 guns, *went back along the Danube's* right bank, but did not take his armour beyond the small town of Amstetten, 125 km west of Vienna. On 4 May his patrols on the outskirts of Linz [on the Danube] met up with the American 3rd Army's. On the Graz road, that same day, they came into contact with British 8th Army reconnaissance parties.'[6]

'The removals van [*cage de fer!*] was waiting at the crossroads. *The two corpses were thrown* on top of the other fifteen. Early in the morning of 29 April 1945 the furniture removals van reached Milan, after passing through several American roadblocks. It stopped in front of an unfinished concrete garage on the Piazzale Loreto.'[7]

'The night of 30 April 1945, Goebbels and Bormann tried vainly to negotiate with the Russians. The answer was: "Unconditional Surrender".'[8]

[1] Latin *tranare* or *transnare:* to journey over, cross. *Tranare flumina curru* (Statius), to cross a river on a chariot or float. D.LAT.

[2] Ancient name for the Danube. Most commentators persist in reading the word as 'Hitler'.

[3] Cf. CIX,Q95, Vol. I.

[4] Latin *infans:* abominable, dreadful. D.LAT.

[5] Typical example of concomitance between two events.

[6] LDG.

[7] MCH.

[8] MAB.

Socialism and François Mitterrand. The First Steps in the Rise to Power

La belle rose[1] en la France admirée,
D'un très grand Prince[2] à la fin désirée,
Six cens et dix, lors naistront ses amours
Cinq ans après, sera d'un grand blessée,[3]
Du trait d'Amour,[4] elle sera enlassée,[5]
Si à quinze du Ciel reçoit secours.

Sixain 44

Interpretation

The fine rose [of Socialism] will be admired in France and its great leader [Mitterrand] shall be sought after at last. At the end of just over fifty years his passion [for the State] will be born. Five years later Socialism will be impressed by a great man [Mitterrand] and will not be harmed by the critics [political attacks], since after fifteen years he will receive Heaven's aid [Jews and Catholics].

History

1916: François Mitterrand born; 610 months = 50 years; 1916 + 50 = 1966. 'On 5 May 1966, François Mitterrand announced the formation of an alternative government similar to the British Shadow Cabinet.'[6]

1966 + 5 = 1971. On 16 June 1971, the new French Socialist Party under Mitterrand's leadership was formed.

1966 + 15 years = 1981. On 10F18 AY 1981, François Mitterrand was elected President of the Republic. 'Of the 1,100,000 vote margin Giscard lost by, at least 500,000 came from the under-21s. The other 60,000 may have expressed the views of discontented minority groups – those Catholics who abstained because of the abortion issue; Jews affected by Yasser Arafat [du Ciel]. . . .'[7]

[1] Cf. CII,Q97 and CV,Q96, Vol. I.
[2] Latin princeps: leader, chief. D.LAT.
[3] To make an impression on. DL7V.
[4] Arrow or shaft of love: what causes a deadly wound. DL7V.
[5] Latin in lassus: not tired, not exhausted.
[6] VCAHU.
[7] Le Spectacle du Monde, no. 231, June 1981.

Nostradamus' Prophecy Carried Worldwide by the Media, 1981. The Aim of the Prophecy

Le divin Verbe[1] donra[2] à la substance,[3]
Comprins ciel, terre, or[4] occult au laict[5] mistique,[6]
Corps, ame, esprit ayant tout puissance,
Tant soubz ses pieds comme au siège Célique.[7]

CIII,Q2

Interpretation

The prophecy will give to [man's spiritual] substance, on earth as in heaven [through radio, television and the press] what was previously hidden in symbolic form, showing that mind and soul have power over the body, as much upon earth as in the Vatican.

[1] Referring to his divine inspiration, Nostradamus here denotes prophecy, the word of God.
[2] For donnera. Example of syncope.
[3] Said of spiritual as opposed to corporeal beings. DL.
[4] For ore, i.e. alors, then.
[5] Symbolic of the first nourishment of the spirit. DL7V.
[6] Symbolizing reference to religious matters. DL7V.
[7] Nostradamus refers to the Catholic Church through the word Ciel, (heaven or sky), with a capital C, and to the Vatican by the word siège (seat), because of the Holy Seat.

The Prophecy of Nostradamus Attacked by the Clergy, 1981

Le divin verbe sera du Ciel frappé
Qui ne pourra procéder plus avant:
Du resserant[1] le secret estoupé,[2]
Qu'on marchera par-dessus[3] et devant.[4]

CII,Q27

Interpretation

The prophecy will be attacked by [the men of] the Church, who could do no more against it. They will want to suppress the decoder's secret, insulting and preceding him [in criticism].

History and commentary

The two quatrains above could possibly refer to the first volume of my work and the phenomenal interest it aroused in Nostradamus' prophecy. I shall therefore make no further comment.

[1] Latin *reserare:* to discover, unveil, reveal. D.LAT.
[2] *Estouper* or *estoper:* to close someone's mouth. DAFL.
[3] To trample upon, insult. DL7V.
[4] To walk ahead of, precede. DL7V.

NOSTRADAMUS AS PROPHET

SUBJECTS OF THE QUATRAINS AND SIXAINS
The Third World War

Egypt's Act of Aggression against a Soviet Ally – Surprise Attack upon West Germany

Invasion by the Warsaw Pact – The Vladivostok Fleet – Replacement of the French Head of State

Invasion of South-west France

Earthquake at Rome between 20 April and 20 May - Collapse of the Colosseum – Moslem Holy War

The Communist System versus Religious Marriages – A Young Moslem Leader Reviled – Political Discussions in Great Britain

Henri the Great and England

Invasion of Italy – Difficulties between France and England–Alliance of France and Spain

The Traditionalists Imprisoned – The Great Monarch Confronted with Revolution

The Revolt of Monsignor Lefèbvre – Triumph of France

Outmoded Anticlericalism Opposed by the Great Monarch

Invasion of Southern Europe in February – Spain Attacked on Three Sides – Invasion of Switzerland

An Army Follows the Paris-Spain Motorway – Flight of the Inhabitants of the Ancona Region – Reinforcements by Land and Sea

Fighting at Port-de-Bouc – Sack of Provence

The Russian Army Besieged in Dôle – Russian Forces Pass through West Germany, Switzerland and Yugoslavia – Invasion of Italy

Great Drought in Southern Countries – Earthquake in Japan – Difficulties between Greece and Turkey

---

Egypt's Act of Aggression against a Soviet Ally. Surprise Attack upon West Germany

> De coup de fer tout le monde estonné,
> Par Crocodil[1] estrangement donné,
> A un bien grand parent de la sangsue,[2]
> Et peu après sera un autre coup
> De guet à pens commis contre le loup,
> Et de tels faits on ne verra l'issue.
>
> Sixain 45

Interpretation

There will be worldwide surprise at an act of war committed by Egypt against an ally of the USSR [Libya, Iran, Syria . . . ?] and shortly afterwards there will be an attack on Germany; no solution to such a situation can be envisaged.

[1] The most ancient species is the Nile crocodile, which the Egyptians used to worship. DL7V. Cf. Sixain 31, Vol. 1.

[2] The leech is a blood-drinker. Denotes the revolutionary USSR. Cf. Sixains 21, 30, 40 and 46, Vol. 1.

Invasion by the Warsaw Pact. The Vladivostok Fleet. Replacement of the French Head of State

Le camp Ascop[1] d'Europe partira,
S'adjoignant proche de l'isle[2] submergée:
D'Arton[3] classe phalange pliera,[4]
Nombril du monde[5] plus grand voix subrogée.[6]

CII,Q22

Interpretation

The Warsaw Pact forces will leave from [Eastern] Europe to link up and invade England. The fleet will deploy its forces from Vladivostok. The head of government will be replaced in Paris.

[1] Anagram of PO(L)SCA, Poland. 'The camp of Ascop' = Warsaw Pact.
[2] Used to denote England, British Isles.
[3] Artom: town near Vladivostok, the main Russian naval base. AU.
[4] For dépliera by aphesis.
[5] Umbilicus Graeciae, the centre of Greece. D.LAT. The centre of the world where one happens to be: i.e. Paris, for Nostradamus.
[6] Latin subrogare: to substitute, name in one's place. D.LAT.

Invasion of South-west France

Les artomiques[1] par Agen et l'Estore,[2]
A sainct Felix[3] feront leur Parlement:
Ceux de Basas[4] viendront à la mal'heure,
Saisir Condon et Marsan promptement.

CIV,Q72

Interpretation

The Soviet forces will pass through Agen and Lectoure and will establish control in the Gironde. Those who will have landed at Bazas will come at a bad time and swiftly occupy Condom and Mont-de-Marsan.

[1] Inhabitants of Artom, near Vladivostok: the Soviets.
[2] For Lectoure: town in the Gers department. Cf. CI,Q79, Vol. I.
[3] Saint's day: 12 February. Perhaps St Felix-de-Foncaude in the Langon district.

⁴ Bazas: parish in the Gironde, in the Langon district. Cf. CI, Q90; CXII,Q65; CI,Q79, all Vol. I.

Earthquake at Rome between 20 April and 20 May. Collapse of the Colosseum. Moslem Holy War

Sol vingt de Taurus¹ si fort terre trembler,
Le grand théâtre² remply ruynera:
L'air ciel et terre obscurcir et troubler,
Lors l'infidèle³ Dieu et saincts voquera.⁴

CIX,Q83

Interpretation

When the sun is in the sign of Taurus, the earth will shake so badly that Rome will be destroyed; the air, sky and earth will be darkened [eclipse] and affected by revolution, and then the Moslems will invoke God and the saints.

¹ The Sun enters Taurus on 20 April (until 20 May). DL7V. In this use of the word Taurus Nostradamus may also be alluding to the mountain range in Turkey.
² The Colosseum is the amphitheatre of Rome. DHD. As he often does elsewhere, Nostradamus here uses a part to denote the whole.
³ Nostradamus' word for the Moslem world in general. Cf. Letter to Henri, and CVIII,Q96, Vol. I.
⁴ Example of aphesis. The Moslem Holy War (or Jehad) is launched with the cry of 'Allah akhbar', 'God is great.'

The Communist System versus Religious Marriages. A Young Moslem Leader Reviled. Political Discussions in Great Britain.

Par le despit¹ nopces, epithalame,²
Par les trois parts Rouges, Razez partis:³
Au jeune noir⁴ remis⁵ par flamme à l'ame,
Au grand Neptune⁶ Ogmius⁷ converti.

Presage 39, May

Interpretation

During a time of contempt for marriage and its ceremonies, the Reds will split up into three sections; the tonsured ones [the Traditionalists] having gone. A young Moslem leader [Col. Gaddafy?] will be rejected because of his inflammatory attitude when the system based on political discourse has been adopted in England.

¹ *Mépris*, scorn or contempt. DAFL.
² Epithalamium: nuptial poem composed in honour of the married couple, which in ancient times was set to music. DL7V.
³ Cf. material concerning the 'tonsured ones' in Vol. I, p. 292 ff.
⁴ Cf. CIII,Q60, Vol. I.
⁵ *Remettre:* to reject, vomit up. DAFL.
⁶ God of the Sea, always used to denote Great Britain.
⁷ Ogmius: god of eloquence and poetry for the Gauls. Denotes the democratic system born in eighteenth-century France. Cf. the poems of Lamartine; also CIX, Q89 and CV, Q80, Vol. I.

Henri the Great and England

Dedans les Isles de cinq fleuves¹ à un,
Par le croissant du grand Chyren Selin:²
Par les bruynes de l'air fureur de l'un,
Six eschapez, cachez fardeaux de lyn.³

CVI,Q27

Interpretation

In the British Isles, which will have been reduced from five rivers to one [the Thames], Great Henri, through his fight against the Crescent, will show his rage because of drizzles from the air [fallout or chemical warfare?], six persons having escaped by hiding in the cargo of a ship.

¹ The major rivers of the British (colonial) Empire were: the Nile, the Ganges, the Indus, the Niger and the Thames = 5.
² Cf. CII,Q79; CIV,Q34; CVI,Q27; CVI,Q70; CVIII,Q54; CIX,Q41, all Vol. I.
³ Or *lin, lein, ligne* = ship, vessel. DAFL.

Invasion of Italy. Difficulties between France and England. Alliance of France and Spain

Terre Italique près des monts tremblera,
Lyon et Coq non trop confederez,
En lieu de peur l'un l'autre s'aydera,
Seul Catulon et Celtes moderez.

CI,Q93

Interpretation

Italian territory will tremble [tank divisions] near the Alps. England and the King of France will not be too friendly. But one shall help the other out of fear. Only the King of Spain and the French will show wisdom.[1]

[1] Cf. CI,Q31; CVIII,Q48 and the Letter to Henri.

The Traditionalists Imprisoned. The Great Monarch Confronted with Revolution

Bruit sera vain, le defaillans troussez,
Les Razes[1] pris: esleu le Pempotan[2]
Faillir deux Rouges et quatre bien croisez,
Pluye[3] empeschable au Monarque potent.[4]

Presage 30, August

Interpretation

Making a noise will be futile, the vanquished will be robbed. The tonsured ones will be imprisoned at the time of an election in England. Two Communist countries [or persons], as well as very Christian countries [or persons], will collapse and revolution will be an obstacle for the powerful monarch.

[1] The Catholic traditionalists or fundamentalists are thus denoted by Nostradamus throughout. Cf. material concerning the 'tonsured ones' in Vol. 1, p. 292 ff.
[2] Cf. CX,Q100, Vol. 1, and CVIII,Q97.
[3] Invariably denotes revolutionary disturbances.
[4] Latin potens: powerful. D.LAT.

The Revolt of Monsignor Lefèbvre. Triumph of France

Armes, playes cesser, mort de séditieux,
Le pere Liber[1] grand non trop abondra[2]
Malins seront saisis par plus malicieux,
France plus que jamais vitrix[3] triomphera.

Presage 127, September

Interpretation

The noise of arms and the disasters of war shall cease the moment a seditious person dies. He who has freed himself from the Pope will not be in full agreement with 'the great one' [the Pope]. The wicked ones shall be trapped by those wilier than themselves. France, more victorious than ever, shall triumph.

[1] *Liber a patre:* freed from paternal authority. D.LAT. Cf. Presage 54, Vol. I.
[2] To be in full agreement with someone, share the same opinion. DL7V.
[3] Latin *victrix:* victorious. D.LAT.

Outmoded Anticlericalism Opposed by the Great Monarch

Yeux clos, ouverts d'antique[1] fantaisie,
L'habit[2] des seuls[3] seront mis à néant:
Le grand monarque chastiera leur frénésie
Ravir des temples le trésor par devant.[4]

CII,QI2

Interpretation

The blind [in spirit] will lay themselves open to outdated fantasies. The priests shall be despoiled of their habitations. The great monarch will chastise their anger by pillaging the treasures of the churches in their presence.

[1] Used ironically for ancient or outworn. DL7V.
[2] The term used by the Fontevrault Order for the lodgings of male clergy, as opposed to *monastère*, referring to nuns' dwellings.

[3] Allusion to celibacy of clergy.
[4] In the presence of. DL7V.

Invasion of Southern Europe in February. Spain Attacked on Three Sides. Invasion of Switzerland

Saturne[1] en Cancer, Jupiter[2] avec Mars,
Dedans Février Caldondon[3] salvaterre:[4]
Sault Castallon[5] assailly de trois pars,
Pres de Verbiesque[6] conflit, mortelle guerre.

CVIII,Q48

Interpretation

Wellbeing shall be replaced by misery, war will be waged upon God [the Church]. In February, from Trento to Lisbon, Spain shall be attacked on three sides, the fighting being near Verbier; this will be a deadly war.

[1] The Golden Age.
[2] Father or master of Heaven, i.e. God.
[3] For Caldonazzo, small Italian town near Trento, on the Innsbruck-Bologna-Milan motorway.
[4] Salvaterra de Magos: small town near Lisbon.
[5] Castulon: town in Tarragona area. Cf. CI,Q31 and CI,Q93.
[6] For Verbier, by paragoge. Small Swiss town in the Valais, on the Milan-Lausanne road.

An Army Follows the Paris-Spain Motorway. Flight of the Inhabitants of the Ancona Region. Reinforcements by Land and Sea

De Sens,[1] d'Autun[2] viendront jusques au Rosne,
Pour passer outre vers les monts Pyrennées,
La gent sortir de la marque d'Anconne,[3]
Par terre et mer suivra à grand trâinées.[4]

CII,Q74

Interpretation

From Sens, passing through Autun [the invasion army] will descend the Rhône valley to reach Spain, over the Pyrenees. The population will flee from the Ancona region, for the land and sea convoys will arrive in strength.

[1] Town in the Yonne department.
[2] Town in the Saône-et-Loire department. Both these towns are on the Paris-Marseille motorway.
[3] Town in the Marches, on the Adriatic Sea.
[4] Long line scored or marked on a surface or in space. DL7V.

Fighting at Port-de-Bouc. Sack of Provence

> La tour marine[1] trois fois prise et reprise,
> Par Espagnols, Barbares, Ligurins:
> Marseille et Aix, Arles par ceux de Pise,
> Vast, feu, fer pillè Avignon des Thurins.[2]
>
> CI,Q71

Interpretation

Port-de-Bouc will be captured and recaptured three times, by the Spanish Army, by Moslem troops and by forces coming from Italy. Marseille, Aix and Arles will be seized by the troops from Pisa who will bring devastation, fire and war, and Avignon will be sacked by the East Germans.

[1] Cf. CI,Q28, Vol. I.
[2] Thuringia, ancient area of central Germany, occupied the area known as Upper Saxony. DHB. Now the province of Thüringen in East Germany; its main town is Weimar.

The Army Besieged in Dôle. Russian Forces Pass through West Germany, Switzerland and Yugoslavia. Invasion of Italy

Le Duc de Langres[1] assiégé dedans Dôle[2]
Accompagné d'Ostun[3] et Lyonnois:
Genève, Auspurg[4] joint ceux de Mirandole[5]
Passer les monts[6] contre les Anconnois.[7]

CVII,Q4

Interpretation

The general from Langres shall be besieged in Dôle, where the armies from Autun and Lyon will have rejoined him, besieged by the armies from Geneva and Augsburg, which will link up with the army that has arrived at Mirandola, after crossing the Alps to march upon Ancona.

[1] Town of the Côte d'Or, north of Dijon.
[2] Town in the Jura, north-west of Chalon-sur-Saône.
[3] For Autun.
[4] For Augsburg, town in West Germany.
[5] Italian town between Modena and Mantua, part of the Duchy of Modena.
[6] The Carnic Alps. Cf. CII,Q32. Vol. I.
[7] Town on the Adriatic coast south-east of Mirandola.

Great Drought in Southern Countries. Earthquake in Japan. Difficulties between Greece and Turkey

Mars[1] et Mercure,[2] et l'argent joint ensemble,
Vers le Midy[3] extrême siccité:
Au fond d'Asie on dira terre tremble,
Corinthe,[4] Éphèse[5] lors en perplexité.

CIII,Q3

Interpretation

When war, pillage and money rule together, there shall be a great drought in the countries of the south. When the earth trembles in Japan, there will be problems between Greece and Turkey.

¹ God of war.
² God of thieves. Hermes in Greek mythology.
³ Allusion to the north-south dialogue. The *Midi* refers in particular to the Moslem countries from Morocco to the Persian or Arabian Gulf.
⁴ Corinth: Greek town of the Peloponnese on the Gulf of Corinth. AVL.
⁵ Ephesus: town in Asia Minor, today in Turkey. AVL.

Earthquakes. The War Spreads to Greece and Turkey

Dans plusieurs nuits la terre tremblera
Sur le printemps, deux efforts¹ feront suite
Corinthe,² Éphèse,³ aux deux mers nagera,⁴
Guerre s'esmeut⁵ par deux vaillants de luite.⁶

CII,Q52

Interpretation

The earth will tremble for several nights, in the spring, two military offensives will follow each other; from Corinth to Ephesus between two seas [Ionian and Aegean] they shall swim, the war being set in motion by two military men.

¹ By extension: the employment of physical or moral action, making an effort to drive back the enemy. DL7V.
² Greek town on the Gulf of Corinth, which borders the Ionian Sea.
³ Turkish town on the Aegean.
⁴ Allusion to sinking ships. Cf. CII,Q60, Vol. I.
⁵ *Esmouvoir:* to set in motion. DAFL.
⁶ For *lutte*, struggle. DAFL.

Origins of the King of France. The Far East Shaken by the War

De l'aquatique triplicité¹ naistra,
D'un qui fera le Jeudy² pour sa feste,
Son bruit, los,³ regne, sa puissance croistra,
Par terre et mer aux Oriens tempeste.

CI,Q50

Interpretation

[The King of France] will be born in Great Britain and adopt Maundy Thursday as his name day. His fame, power and reputation will grow, when the countries of Asia [China and Japan] are shaken by war on land and sea.

  [1] Whatever is triple or tripartite. DL. Reference to Neptune's trident: the sea god invariably denotes Great Britain.
  [2] Maundy Thursday, the Thursday of Holy Week. DL.
  [3] Praise, honour, glory. DAFL.

Flight into Spain by a Head of State. Fighting in the Alps. His Reign in Peace

L'un des plus grands fuyra aux Espagnes
Qu'en longue playe après viendra seigner,
Passant copies[1] par les hautes montagnes,
Dévastant tout, et puis en paix régner.

                              CIII,Q54

Interpretation

One of the greatest men shall flee to Spain, after which a long wound [war] will bleed. He will get troops across the Alps,[2] devastating all [tactical nuclear weapons?], and then reign in peace.

  [1] Latin *copiae:* army corps, troops, military forces. D.LAT.
  [2] Cf. cx,Q37, Vol. I.

Subversion in the Toulouse Region. Restoration of Liberties by the Bourbon

Le regne[1] et loy sous Venus[2] eslevé,[3]
Saturne[4] qui a sus Jupiter[5] empire
La loy et régne par le Soleil levé[6]
Par Saturnins[7] endurera le pire.

                              CV,Q24

Interpretation

The power and the law which had been taken away by subversion, before the Golden Age is to establish its empire over the world, will be restored by the Bourbon, for the worst will be endured because of the inhabitants of Toulouse.

   [1] Latin *regnum:* power, strength. DLLB.
   [2] Used by Nostradamus to denote subversion.
   [3] Latin *elevare:* to take away, deprive. DLLB.
   [4] The time of Saturn and Rhea, the Golden Age which will last as long as Saturn governs the universe. DL7V.
   [5] God of Heaven and Earth. DL7. Cf. CIV, Q33, Vol. I.
   [6] Example of aphesis: *levé* for *relevé.*
   [7] Saturnin or Sernin: disciple from Languedoc and first Bishop of Toulouse. DL7V. Nostradamus uses the name as a sort of code or shorthand for the inhabitants of Toulouse.

Link-up with the American Forces at Savona. Hungary Leaves the Warsaw Pact and Joins NATO and Japan. Liberation of Italy

Pendant que l'Aigle[1] et le Coq[2] à Savone
Seront unis, Mer,[3] Levant[4] et Ongrie;
L'armée à Naples, Palerme, Marque d'Ancone,
Rome, Venise par Barbe[5] horrible crie.

CVIII, Q9

Interpretation

While the forces of the [American] Eagle and the Cock [King of France] are reunited at Savona, as well as with the Atlantic Alliance, Japan and Hungary, the Army shall reach Naples, Palermo and Ancona, at which time in Rome and Venice the [red] republic shall provoke cries of horror.

   [1] Cf. CVIII,Q4, Vol. I.
   [2] The first medal upon which the cock emblem appeared was struck in 1601, upon the birth of Louis XIII. The future king of France was thus designated to stress his origin from the senior branch of the Bourbons.
   [3] By analogy: vast space or area. DL7V. Nostradamus thus alludes to the *Atlantic* Alliance, extending from the USA as far as Turkey. Note the capital M.

[4] *Soleil levant*, i.e. the rising sun, Japan.
[5] Cf. CIX,Q6, Vol. I.

The Red Army's Retreat through Greece. The Western Countries Return in Strength

L'ennemi tant à craindre retirer en Thracie,[1]
Laissant cris, hurlemens, et pille desolée:
Laisser bruit mer et terre, religion murtrie,
Joviaux mis[2] en route, toute sects affoulée.

Presage 129, November

Interpretation

The enemy so feared will retreat in Greece, leaving behind cries, screams and desolation through pillage, noise by land and sea, and religion wounded; then those of the West will mobilize and the political parties will be terror-stricken.

[1] Thrace: north-eastern part of Greece.
[2] Jovial, i.e. pertaining to Jove or Jupiter. D. LAT. The planet Jupiter was regarded by astrologers as a source of good fortune. DL7V. Nostradamus here denotes the West and its wellbeing. Cf. Presage 32, Vol. I.

Collapse of the Soviet Empire. French Revival. New Alliances

Sangsuë en peu de temps mourra,
Sa mort bon signe nous donra,
Pour l'accroissement de la France,
Alliance se trouveront,
Deux grands Royaumes se joindront,
François aura sur eux puissance.

Sixain 58

Interpretation

The USSR shall crumble and that will be good for France's new growth. Alliances will be made. Two great countries will unite under the influence of France.

Communism Abandoned in Seven Countries. Homage Paid to the King of France and Navarre

> Le procrée naturel dogmion[1]
> De sept à neuf du chemin destourner,
> A roy de longue[2] et amy au my[3] hom.
> Doit à Navarre fort de Pau[4] prosterner.

> CVIII,Q44

Interpretation

The natural heir to the system based upon political discourses [the Communism stemming from the parliamentary system born in 1789 with the Oath of the Tennis Court] will cease in seven countries out of nine, because of him who will become king after a long while, and for whom there will be friendship among men, who should bow down before the powerful person from Pau, King of France and of Navarre.

[1] Several editions have '*d'ogmion*' or '*d'Ogmion*'. Cf. Presage 39; and in Vol. 1 cv,Q80 and cix,Q89.
[2] Feminine ending, for '*longue durée*', i.e. of time. DL7V.
[3] *A my* or *a mi*, meaning amid. DAFL.
[4] Henri V, successor of Henri IV whose birthplace was Pau.

World Wars. Return of the Monarchy

> Tant d'ans en Gaule les guerres dureront,
> Outre la course de Castulon[1] monarque:
> Victoire incerte trois grands couronneront,
> Aigle,[2] coq,[3] Lune,[4] Lyon,[5] Soleil en marque.

> CI,Q31

Interpretation

Wars will last in France for many years, after the reign of the King of Spain. Three heads of states [USA, France and England] will celebrate an indecisive victory. The USA, the King of France, the Republic, England will see the sign of the monarchy.

  [1] Castulon, town in Tarragona, today Carbona. DLLB. Tarragona was one of the three great provinces of ancient Spain, and consisted approximately of the modern provinces of Catalonia, Aragon, Navarre, Biscay, Asturias, Galicia, Minho and Douro, Tras-os-Montes, Leon, Old (and some of New) Castile, and Valencia. DHB. Nostradamus, as he often does, denotes the King of Spain by referring to a small town within the chief province of that country. Cf. cv, Q99, Vol. i, and cviii,Q9.
  [2] The American Eagle. Cf. cv,Q99, Vol. i, and cviii,Q9.
  [3] Cf. pp. 388–89, Vol. i.
  [4] Taken as symbol of the Republic, as opposed to the Sun, symbol of the Monarchy.
  [5] The British Lion.

Peace Returns. Union of France and Spain

Croix paix, soubs un accomply divin verbe,
Espagne et Gaules seront unis ensemble:
Grand clade[1] proche, et combat tres acerbe,
Coeur si hardy ne sera qui ne tremble.

CIV,Q5

Interpretation

The Christians [Catholics and Protestants] will be at peace; God's word [the prophecy] will be fulfilled. Spain and France shall be united, after a major defeat and a very bitter war affects them, so much so that even the most courageous will tremble.

  [1] Latin *clades:* loss, calamity, disaster – especially of a military reverse or defeat. D.LAT.

SUBJECTS OF THE QUATRAINS AND SIXAINS

The Yellow Invasion – 1999

The Yellow Invasion Preceded by the Russian Revolution

The End of the 'Western Era' – Quarrels among the Theologians

The End of Communism in Russia – The USSR Besieged by the Eastern Bloc (China, Japan) – The Golden Age

Disastrous Harvests – Appalling Climatic Conditions – Asia (Japan and China) Arms – France Besieged

The Vatican Ravaged by the Asiatic States (China and Japan)

Scotland, then England, Attacked by the Yellow Peril

The Fall of the Asiatic Empire – Danger at Salon in Provence

The End of Wars – The First Resurrection

Universal Peace for a Thousand Years – The First Resurrection, 2026–3000

The Yellow Invasion Preceded by the Russian Revolution

> Beaucoup avant telles menées,[1]
> Ceux d'Orient par la vertu Lunaire:
> L'an mil sept cents seront grand emmenées,[2]
> Subjugant presque le coing Aquilonnaire.
>
> CI,Q49

Interpretation

Well before such great attacks coming from Asia by a Republican system [People's Republic of China], in the year 1917 the great ones [Tsar and his family] will be carried off [by the Revolution] which will put Russia under its yoke.

[1] Charge, attack, pursuit. DAFL.
[2] Cf. Presages 62 and 89, Vol. I.

The End of the 'Western Era'. Quarrels among the Theologians

Le temps présent avecques le passé,
Sera jugé par le grand Jovialiste:[1]
Le monde tard par luy sera lassé,
Et desloyal par le clergé juriste.

CX,Q73

Interpretation

The great leader of the West shall judge the present and the past. He will abandon the [western] world towards its end [1999], the theologians then showing their disloyalty.

[1] Cf. Letter to Henri and Presage 129. Does this refer to the King of France and his end, *c.* 1999?

The Chinese Flood through the West. Subversion in Africa. The Golden Age Comes from Asia

Mer par solaires[1] seure[2] passera,
Ceux de Venus[3] tiendront toute l'Afrique:
Leur Regne plus Saturne[4] n'occupera,
Et changera la part Asiatique.

CV,Q11

Interpretation

The sister of the Japanese [China] will cross the sea. The subversives will be everywhere in Africa. Their power will not last until the Golden Age, since change will come from part of Asia.

[1] The word *solaires* in the plural is only used by Nostradamus in this particular quatrain. He seems here to be referring to the Japanese.
[2] The sister of Japan, China.
[3] Cf. CIV,Q28, Vol. I.
[4] The time of Saturn and Rhea: Golden Age which is to last while Saturn governs the universe. DL7V.

The End of Communism in Russia. The USSR Besieged by the Eastern Bloc (China, Japan). The Golden Age

Froid, grand déluge[1] de regne dechassé,
Niez, discord. Trion[2] crient mine:
Poison, mis siege, de la Cité chassé,
Retour felice, neuve secte en ruine.

Presage 21, October

Interpretation

During the winter the great [October] revolution will be driven out of power because it will have been led by fools who will disagree. The States of Asia will threaten the USSR with chemical warfare; the latter will be besieged. [The Russians] will be driven from Moscow. Then happiness shall return, when the new party [Communist] is in ruins.

[1] Words such as water, wave, whirlpool, flood, typhoon etc. are always used as symbols of revolution.

[2] Trion: astronomical term; Septentrion is the name given to the seven stars forming the constellations of Ursa Major and Minor. DL7V. Allusion to Russia in Europe and Russia in Asia, as well as to the seven Warsaw Pact countries. USSR is called the bear (Latin *ursa*) elsewhere.

Disastrous Harvests. Appalling Climatic Conditions. Asia (Japan and China) Arms. France Besieged

Les bleds trop n'abonder, de toutes autres fruits,
L'esté, printemps humide, hiver long, neige, force,[1] glace:
En armes l'Orient, la France se renforce,
Mort de bestail prou miel, aux assiegez la place.

Presage 124, June

Interpretation

Wheat will be in short supply. Among all the other fruits of the earth, violence will predominate. After a rainy spring and summer there will be a long, snowy, glacial winter. The Orient will arm itself, France reinforce herself. The death of cattle will put an end to prosperity for those besieged in their own land [France].

¹ Forcing, in agricultural terms, *forceis:* force, power, violence. DAFL.

The Vatican Ravaged by the Asiatic States (China and Japan)

En débats Princes et Chrestienté esmeuë,
Gentils¹ estranges, siege à Christ molesté:
Venu tres mal, prou² bien, mortelle veue.
Mort Orient peste, faim, mal³ traité.

Presage 83, April

Interpretation

When there are discussions between heads of state and Christianity is agitated, the seat of Christianity [the Vatican] will be tormented by brave foreigners. This will be very untimely, under cover of benevolence, and will turn out to be fatal. The Orient will bring death, calamity and famine, because of a bad treaty.

¹ Valiant, generous. DAFL.
² *Pour*, for. DAFL.
³ Bad, wicked. DAFL.

Scotland, then England, attacked by the Yellow Peril

Soubs le terroir du rond globe lunaire,¹
Lors que sera dominateur Mercure,²
L'Isle d'Écosse³ sera un luminaire,⁴
Qui les Anglois mettra à déconfiture.

CV,Q93

Interpretation

Under the jurisdiction of the great Yellow Empire run by a rogue, Scotland will be in flames and after that the English will be discomfited.

¹ Allusion to sallow hue of the Asiatics. Cf. CVI,Q80, Vol. I.

² God of thieves. Ambassador plenipotentiary to the gods, he presided over alliances and treaties, sanctioning and ratifying them, and was no stranger to declarations of war between cities and nations. MGR. Cf. CX,Q75, Vol. I.

³ Cf. CX,Q66, Vol. I.

⁴ Symbolic. For *flambeau*, torch. DL7V.

The Fall of the Asiatic Empire. Danger at Salon in Provence

Quand seront proches le défaut des lunaires,¹
De l'un à l'autre ne distant grandement,
Froid, siccité, dangers sur les frontières,
Mesme où l'oracle a pris commancement.

CIII,Q4

Interpretation

When the fall of the Asiatic armies is near, it will not be long between their peak and their fall.² There will be cold, drought and various dangers on the frontiers, even where the prophecy began [at Salon in Provence].

¹ Cf. CV,Q93.
² Cf. CVIII,Q77, Vol. I.

The End of Wars. The First Resurrection

Les os des pieds et des mains enserrez,¹
Par bruit maison longtemps inhabitée,
Seront par songes² concavant³ deterrez,
Maison salubre et sans bruit habitée.

CVII,Q41

Interpretation

Those whose skeletons were enclosed and who had left their houses a long time uninhabited because of the noise [of war] shall leave their tombs in their sleep and shall inhabit a healthy house without noise [of war].

¹ To lock away, enclose, shut in. DAFL.
² In dream, during sleep. DL7V.
³ Latin *concavare:* to make hollow, hollow out, empty. D. LAT. The present participle is used here as a noun.

Universal Peace for a Thousand Years. The First Resurrection, 2026–3000

Au revole¹ du grande nombre septiesme,²
Apparoistra au temps jeux d'Hécatombe:³
Non esloigné du grand eage milliesme,⁴
Que les entrez sortiront de leur tombe.

CX,Q74

Interpretation

When the seventh millennium is reached [7000=2000] there shall then be a veritable hecatomb which will happen close to the millennium [1999]. Then those who entered the tomb shall leave it.

Comparison with Revelations 20: 1–5

And I saw an angel come down from heaven, having the key of the bottomless pit and a great chain in his hand.

And he laid hold on the dragon, that old serpent, which is the Devil, and Satan, and bound him *a thousand years.*⁵

And cast him into the bottomless pit, and shut him up, and set a seal upon him, that he should deceive the nations no more, till the thousand years should be fulfilled [the year 3000]: and after that he must be loosed a little season.

And I saw thrones, and they sat upon them, and judgement was given unto them: and I saw the souls of them that were beheaded for the witness of Jesus, and for the word of God,⁶ and which had not worshipped the beast, neither his image, neither had received his mark upon their foreheads, or in their hands; and *they lived*⁵ and reigned with Christ *a thousand years.*⁵

But the rest of the dead lived not again until the thousand years were finished. This is the first resurrection.

[1] Latin *revolutus:* having made its revolution, passed.
[2] Cf. CI,Q48, Vol. I.
[3] Great public sacrifice, the number and type of victims unspecified. DL7V.
[4] According to Nostradamus, this thousand-year period begins in 2026, not 2000.
[5] Author's italics.
[6] For Nostradamus, the Word of God is prophecy. Cf. CII, Q27 and CIII,Q2.

BIBLIOGRAPHY

Abbreviations

BN: Bibliothèque Nationale
BMA: Bibl. Municipale Aix-en-Provence
BML: Bibl. Municipale Lyon

Allaines, Henri d': *Actualité de l'Apocalypse*, La Colombe, Paris, 1963.
Alleau, René: 'Nostradamus le plus grand prophète de l'histoire', *Sallonensa*, Salon, 1957.
Alliaume, Maurice: *Magnus Rex de Nostradamus et son drapeau*, publ. at author's expense at Chartres, 1948.
   Prédictions vraies de Nostradamus et Mandragore, publ. at author's expense at Chartres, 1949.
Amadou, Robert: 'Le Devin et son Art', *Le Crapouillot*, no. 18, 1952.
Amiaux: *Nostradamus*, Sorlot, Paris.
Anon: *La Première Invective du Seigneur Hercules, Le François, contre Nostradamus*, Michel Jove, Lyon, 1558.
   Huictain contre Nostradamus, Roux, Lyon, 1557.
   Déclaration des abus, ignorances, séditions de Michel Nostradamus, Pierre Roux et Jean Tremblay, Avignon, 1558.
Anquetil, Georges: *L'Anti-Nostradamus*, Ed. de la Maison des Ecrivains, Paris, 1940.
Artigny, Abbéd': *Nouveaux mémoires d'histoire, de critique et de littérature*, 1794.
Astruc, Jean: *Mémoires pour servir à l'histoire de la faculté de Montpellier*, 1767.
Auclair, Raoul: *Les Centuries de Nostradamus*, Deux Rives, Paris, 1958.
   Le Crépuscule des Nations, La Colombe, Paris.
   Les Centuries de Nostradamus ou le dixième livre sibyllin, Nouvelles Editions Latines, 1957.
Barbarin, Georges: *Les Derniers Temps du Monde, de l'Antéchrist au Jugement dernier*, 'History & Tradition' series, Ed. Dervy, Paris, 1951.
Bareste, Eugène: Editions des Centuries, Maillet, Paris, 1840–42. (BMA)
Bartoshek, Norbert: *Nostradamus und seine berühmte Prophezeiungen*, 1946.
Belland, Dr: *Napoléon, premier empereur des français, prédit par Nostradamus*, Paris, 1806.

Beltikhine, G.: 'Un document chiffré: Le Secret des Centuries', *Inconnues*, no. 12, Lausanne, 1956.

Bertrand, Michel: 'Histoire secréte de la Provence', *Histoire secrète des provinces françaises*, Albin Michel, Paris, 1978.

Bjorndahl-Veggerby, Paul: *Nostradamus et les ruines gallo-romaines à Martres-Tolosane*, Ed. Leisner, Copenhagen, 1976.

Blanchard and Reynaud-Plense: *La Vie et l'Oeuvre de Michel Nostradamus*, Imp. Léon Guillaumichon, Salon, 1933. (BMA)
Histoire de Salon, Salon, 1935.

Boniface, A: *Buonaparte prédit par des prophètes et peint par des historiens, des orateurs et des poètes ou morceaux en prose et en vers sur les circonstances actuelles, receuillis par A. Boniface*, d'Hautel, Paris, 1814.

Bonnelier, Hippolyte: *Nostradamus, roman historico-cabalistique*, A. Ledoux, Paris, 1833, 2 vol.

Bonnet, Jean: *Résumé des Prophéties de Nostradamus. Les événements et les symboles*, followed by: *Commentaires de la Bible par Nostradamus et de détermination des dates dans Nostradamus*, Jean Bonnet, Paris, 1973.

Bonnot, Jean de: *Les Oracles de Michel de Nostredame dit Nostradamus*, annotated by Anatole le Pelletier and Serge Hutin, 1976, 2 vol.

Boroch, Erich Karl: *Der Prophet Nostradamus*, 1912.

Boswell, Rolfe: *Nostradamus speaks*, 1941.

Bouche, Honoré: *La Chorographie et l'Histoire de Provence*, Charles David, Aix-en-Provence, 1664.

Bouchet, Marguerite: *Les Oracles de Michel de Nostredame*, Les Livres Nouveaux, Paris, 1939.

Boulenger, Jacques: *Nostradamus*, Excelsior, Paris, 1933.

Bousquet, Raoul: *Nostradamus, sa famille et son secret*, Fournier-Valdes, Paris, 1950.
'La Maladie et la Mort de Nostradamus', *Aesculape*, November 1950.

Boutin, André: *Michel de Nostre-Dame, astrologue et médecin*, MD thesis, Librairie Le François, Paris, 1941.

Bouys, Théodore: *Nouvelles considérations sur les Oracles et particulièrement sur Nostradamus*, Paris, 1806, Desenne, Debray.

Boyer, Jean: 'Deux peintres oubliés du XVIIᵉ siècle, Etienne Martellange et César Nostradamus', *Bulletin de la Société de l'histoire de l'Art Français, 1971, pp. 13–20*.

Bricaud, Joanny: *La Guerre et les Prophéties célèbres*, Paris, 1916.

Buget, P. F.: 'Etude sur Nostradamus', *Bulletin du bibliophile*, Librairie Techner, Paris, 1860.

Buset, Claude: *Nostradamus et autres prophètes du Père et de l'Esprit*, La Pensée Universelle, Paris, 1974.

Cadres, Geoffroy: *L'Etrange docteur Nostradamus*, La Pensée Universelle, Paris 1978.

Candolle, Comte de: *Armorial de César de Nostredame*, Arles, 1899. (BMA)

Cavanagh, John: *Michel de Nostradamus*, 1923.

Cave, Térence C.: 'Peinture et émotion dans la poésie religieuse de César de Nostredame', *Gazette des Beaux-Arts*, vol. LXXV, Jan. 1970. (BMA)

Centurio, N.: *Nostradamus, der Prophet der Weltgeschichte*, Richar Schikowski, Berlin, 1955.

Chabauty, Abbé E. A.: *Lettres sur les Prophéties modernes et concordance de toutes les prédictions jusqu'au règne de Henry V*, Ed. Henri Houdin, Poitiers, 1872.

Chavigny, A. de: *Les Pléiades du Sieur de Chavigny, Beaunois, divisées en VII livres, prises et tirées des anciennes prophéties et conférées avec les oracles du tant célèbre et renommé Michel de Nostradame, jadis conseiller et médecin de trois Rois très chrestiens. Où est traté du renouvellement des siècles, changement de l'Empire et advancement du nom Chrestien*, Lyon, Pierre Rigaud, 1604.

Chavigny, J. A. de: *Commentaires du Sieur de Chavigny sur les Centuries et Prognostications de feu Michel de Nostredame du Breui*, Paris, 1596.
La première Face du Janus français extraite et colligée des Centuries de Michel Nostradamus, par les héritiers de Pierre Roussin, Lyon, 1594. (BMA)
Vie et testament de Michel Nostradamus, Paris, 1789.
'Bref discours sur la Vie de Michel de Nostredame', *Revue de l'Agenois*, 1876.

Cheetham, Erika: *The Prophecies of Nostradamus*, Capricorn Books, Putnam's, New York, 1973.

Chollier, Antoine: *Les Prophéties de maistre Michel Nostradamus*, Imp. Allier, Grenoble, 1940.

Chomorat, Michel: *Nostradamus entre Rhône et Saône*, Ed. Ger, Lyon, 1971.
Supplément à la bibliographie Lyonnaise des Nostradamus. Central culturel de Buenc, Lyon, 1976. 100 numbered copies.
'New research on the prophecies of M. N.', *Revue française d'histoire du livre*, no. 22, spring 1979.
Bibliographie lyonnaise de Nostradamus, followed by a checklist of MSS relating to the Nostradamus family, Centre Culturel de Buenc, Lyon, 1973.

Colin de Larmor: *La Guerre de 1914–1918 vue en 1555 par Nostradamus*, La Roche-sur-Yon, 1922.
Merveilleux Quatrains de Nostradamus, Nantes, 1925. (BMA)

Colin-Simard: 'Rois et Reines au rendez-vous des astrologues', *Historia*, no. 157, 1959.

Corvaja, Mireille: *Les Prophéties de Nostradamus*, Vecchi, Paris, 1975.

Couillard, Antoine: *Les Contredits aux prophéties de Nostradamus*, Charles l'Angelier, Paris, 1560.

Crescimbeni, Giovanni-Mario: *Istoria della volgar poesia-TII: Le vite de'piu celebri poeti provenzali, scritte in lingua francese da G. M. Crescimbeni. B. U.* Montpellier (see Jean de Nostredame).

Cristiani Chanoine: *Nostradamus, Malachie et Cie*, Le Centurion, 1955.
'Un Curieux Homme: Nostradamus', *Ecclesia*, no. 73, 1955.

Crouzet, François: 'Nostradamus, Poète français', *Idée Fixe*, Julliard, Paris, 1973.

Da Cruz Marques: *Profecias de Nostradamus*, Ed. Cultrix, Sao Paolo.

Daudet, L.: 'Nostradamus', *Revue universelle*, 1925, vol. I. (BMA)

David-Marescot, Yves and Yvonne: *Prédictions et Prophéties*, Ed, Idégraf et Vernoy, Geneva, 1979.

D. D.: *The Prophecies of Nostradamus concerning the kings and queens of Great Britain*, London, 1715.

Delcourt, Marie: *L'Oracle de Delphes*, 1954.
Demar-Latour: *Nostradamus et les Evénements de 1914–1916*, Paris, 1916. (BN)
Deperlas, Félix: *L'Avenir ou les Grands Personnages et les Grands Evénements de ce temps*, Paris, 1885.
Révélations de la Providence, Paris, 1885.
Dupont-Fournieux, Y.: *Les Derniers Jours des Derniers Temps* (Preface by Dr Fontbrune), La Colombe, Paris 1959.
Edouard, P.: *Texte original et complet des Prophéties de Michel Nostradamus*, Les Belles Editions, Paris, 1939.
Edouard and Mezerette: *Texte original des Prophéties de Nostradamus de 1600 à 1948 et de 1948 à l'an 2000*, Les Belles Editions, Paris, 1947.
Erlanger, Ph.: 'La Reine du Massacre', *Historia*, no. 340, March 1975.
Fervan, Jean: *La Fin des temps*, Ed. La Bourdonnais, Paris, 1937.
Fontbrune, Dr Max de: *Les Prophéties de Nostradamus dévoilées. Lettres à Henry Second*, Adyar, 1937.
Les prophéties de Maistre Michel Nostradamus expliquées et commentées, Ed. Michelet, Sarlat, 1938, 1939, 1940, 1946, 1958 & 1975, J. -Ch. de Fontbrune, Aix-en-Provence, distributed by le Groupe des Presses de la Cité.
Fontbrune, Dr Max de: *Ce que Nostradamus a vraiment dit*, Preface by Henry Miller, Ed. Stock, 1976.
Fontbrune, Dr Max de: *La Prédiction mystérieuse de Prémol*, Michelet, Sarlat, 1939, o.p.
La divine Tragédie de Louis XVII, Michelet, Sarlat, 1949, available from J.-Ch. de Fontbrune, 3, cours Gambetta, Aix-en-Provence.
Fontbrune, Dr Max de: *L'Etrange XXe siècle vu par Nostradamus*, Michelet, Sarlat, 1950, o.p.
'Pourquoi je crois en Nostradamus', *Ecclesia*, no. 82, 1956.
'Le docteur Nostradamus vous parle', *Les Cahiers de Marottes et Violons d'Ingres*, no. 10, Paris, 1953.
'Nostradamus', *Synthèses*, no. 3, August 1955.
Foretich, Rodolphe: *La Prophétie des Papes, analysée à la lumière des prédictions de Nostradamus*, Salvador, 1961. (BN)
Forman, Henry-James: *Les Prophéties à travers les siècles*, Payot, 1938.
Frontenac, Roger: *Le Clé secrète de Nostradamus*, Denoël, Paris, 1950.
Fulke: *Contra inutiles Astrologorum praedictiones, Nostradamus*, Cunningham, 1560. (British Museum)
Garçon, Maurice: 'Il y a 450 ans Nostradamus naissait', *Historia*, no. 85, 1953.
Garencieres, Theophilus: *The True Prophecies of Prognostications of Michael Nostradamus*, London, 1672.
Gauquelin, Michel: 'Les Astres ont-ils changé le cours de l'histoire?', *Historia*, no. 203, 1963.
Gay-Rosset, Claude: 'Michel de Nostredame, une rencontre du quatrième type,' *Midi-Mutualité*, no. 12, Marseille, Jan.-Feb. 1979.
Gimon, Louis: *Chroniques de la ville de Salon depuis son origine jusqu'en 1792*, Aix-en-Provence, 1882.
Girard, Samuel: *Histoire généalogique de la Maison de Savoie*, 1660.
Gravelaine, Joëlle de: *Prédictions at Prophéties*, Hachette, Paris, 1965.

Guérin, Pierre: *Le Véritable secret de Nostradamus*, Payot, Paris, 1971.

Guichardan, S.: *La Chasse aux prophéties*, Bonne Presse, Limoges, 1941.

Guichenou, Joseph: *Catalogue de tableaux au musée Calvet*, Avignon, 1909.

Guynaud, Balthazard: *Concordance des prophéties depuis Henri II jusqu'à Louis le Grand*, Jacques Morel, Paris, 1693.

Hades: *Que sera demain?*, La Table Ronde, Paris, 1966.

Haitze, Pierre Joseph de: *La Vie de Nostradamus*, David, Aix-en-Provence, 1712.
Vie et Testament de Nostradamus, 1789.
La Vie de Nostradamus, Aix-en-Provence, 1911.

Harold, R. A.: *Les Prophétes et les Prophéties de l'Apocalypse à nos jours*, Ed. La Caravelle, Brussels; l'Avenir, Paris, 1948.

Hildebrand, Jakob: *Nostradamus Sueddeutsche Monatshefte*, 1932.

Holtzauer, Jean-Louis: *Nostradamus, un praticien sous la Renaissance*, Laboratoires S.O.B.I.O., Ed. Labo, 92-Levallois, 1975.

Hutin, Serge: *Les Prophéties de Nostradamus avec présages et sixains*, Pierre Bellefond, Paris, 1962, 1972, 1978, Poche-Club, Paris, 1966; Hachette, Paris, 1975.
Les Prophéties de Nostradamus, Club Géant Historique, Les éditions de la Renaissance, Paris, 1966.

Iacchia, U.: *La Tunisie vue par Nostradamus*, Imp. d'Art, Tunis.

IAF: *Le Substrat mathématique de l'Oeuvre de Nostradamus*, Ed. de Psyché, Paris, 1949.

I.M.: *Le vrayes centuries de Me Michel Nostradamus expliquées sur les affaires de ce temps*, I. Boucher, 1652.

Ionescu, Vlaicu: *Le Message de Nostradamus sur l'Ere Prolétaire*, publ. at author's expense, distributed by Dervy Books, Paris, 1976.
'Nostradamus et la gnose', *Atlantis*, no. 301, Jan.–Feb. 1979, 30 rue de la Marseillaise, 94300 Vincennes.

Jacquemin, Suzanne: *Les Prophéties des Derniers Temps*, La Colombe, Paris, 1958.

Jant, Chevalier de: *Prédictions tirées des Centuries de Nostradamus qui vraisemblablement peuvent s'expliquer à la guerre entre la France et l'Angleterre contre les provinces unies*, 1673.
Prophéties de Nostradamus sur la longueur des jours et la félicité du règne de Louis XIV, 1673.

Jaubert, Etienne: *Eclaircissement des véritables quatrains de Nostradamus et Vie de M. Nostradamus*, Amsterdam, 1656.

Kerdeland, Jean de: *De Nostradamus à Cagliostro*, Ed. Self, Paris, 1945.

Klinckowstroem, G. C. Von: *Die ältesten Ausgaben des Prophéties des Nostradamus*, March 1913.

Kniepf, Albert: *Die Weissagungen des altfranzösischen Sehers Michel Nostradamus und der Weltkreig*, Hamburg, 1915.

Krafft, Karl E.: *Nostradamus prezice vütorul Européi*, Bucharest, 1941.

Labadie, Jean: *Peut-on dire l'avenir?*, Aubanel, Avignon, 1941.

Lamont, André: *Nostradamus sees all*, 1942.

Lamotte, Pierre: *De Gaulle révélé par Nostradamus il y a quatre siècles*, Le Scorpion, Paris, 1961. (BN)

Langlois, Charles: *Les Contradictions de Nostradamus*, 1560.

Laurent: *Prédictions jusqu'à l'an 2000. Prophéties du Christ, de Nostradamus, des Papes St Malachie*, Laurent, 91 Brunoy.

Laver, James: *Nostradamus*, Penguin Books, 1942.
Nostradamus, the future foretold, George Mann, Maidstone, 1973.

Legrand, Jean René: 'Pronostics pour l'an 1959', *Initiation et science*, no. 47, Jan.–March 1959, Omnium littéraire, Paris.

Leoni, Edgar: *Nostradamus, life and literature*, 1961.

Le Pelletier, Anatole: *Les Oracles de Nostradamus, astrologue, médecin et conseiller ordinaire des rois Henry II, François II et Charles IX*, Le Pelletier, 40, rue d'Aboukir, Paris, 1867, 2 vol.

Le Roux, Jean: *La Clé de Nostradamus, Isagoge ou Introduction au véritable sens des Prophéties de ce fameux auteur*, Pierre Giffard, rue Saint-Jacques-près-les-Maturins, Paris, 1710. (Musée d'Arbaud, Aix-en-Provence)

Leroy, Dr Edgar: 'Les origines de Nostradamus', *Mémoires de l'Institut historique de Provence*, vol. 18, Marseille, 1941.
Sur un quatrain de Nostradamus.
'Jaume de Nostredame et la Tour de Canillac', *Mémoires de l'Institut historique de Provence*, vol. 19, Marseille, 1942.
'Pierre de Nostredame de Carpentras', communication à l'Institut historique de Provence, 1948.
'Nostradamus et le curé d'Argoeuvres', *Cahier de Pratique Médiocochirurgicale*, Avignon, 1939, no. 5.
Saint-Paul de Mausole à Saint-Rémy de Provence, Imp. générale du Sud-Ouest, Bergerac, 1948.
Nostradamus, ses origines, sa vie, son oeuvre, Imp. Trillaud, Bergerac, 1972.
Romanin, les cours d'amour de Jehan de Nostredame, Avignon, 1933. (BMA)
Saint-Rémy de Reims, Marseille, 1937. (BMA)
Nostradamus, détective avant la lettre, Avignon, 1949. (BN)
Le Latin du tabellion provençal Jaume de Nostredame, notaire à Saint-Rémy-de-Provence dans les actes de 1501 à 1513, Avignon, 1961.
'Saint-Paul-Tricastin et Saint-Paul-de-Mausole, Contribution à l'histoire d'une légende', *Bull. Philologique et Historique*, 1959.

Ligeoix-de-la-Combe: *La Troisième Guerre Mondiale d'après les prédictions de Nostradamus*, Bordeaux, 1961.

Loog, C. L.: *Die Weissagungen des Nostradamus*, 1921.

Loroit, Louis: 'Entretien de Rabelais et de Nostradamus', Nogent-Le-Rotrou, 1960 & Paris, 1907, *Revue des Etudes rabelaisiennes*, vol. 5, pp. 176–84.

Mabille, Pierre: 'Nostradamus, ses prophéties, son temps', *Inconnues*, Lausanne, 1955.

Maby, Pascale: 'Le Dossier des Prophétes, voyants et astrologues', *Les Chemins de l'Impossible*, Albin Michel, Paris, 1977.

MacCann, Lee, *Nostradamus, the man who saw through time*, 1941.

MacNeice, Louis: *L'Astrologie*, Tallandier, Paris, 1966.

Madeleine, Georges: *La Prochaine Guerre Mondiale vue par Nostradamus*, Toulon, 1952, Ed. Proventia.

Maidy, Léon-Germain de: *Sur une inscription liminaire attribuée à Nostradamus*, Nancy, 1917.

Marteau, Pierre: *Entretiens de Rabelais et de Nostradamus*, 1690.

Menestrier, François: *La Philosophie des images énigmatiques*, Lyon, 1694.

Mericourt, M. J.: *Gesta Dei per Francos*, Paris, 1937.

Nostradamus et la crise actuelle, Paris, 1937.

Mondovi, Pierre: 'Un Provençal hors du commun: Nostradamus', *Racines*, no. 4, May 1979, Aix-en-Provence.

Monnier: *Résurrection merveilleuse en 1877 de Michel de Nostredame*, various pamphlets from 1889 to 1896.

Monterey, Jean: *Nostradamus, prophète du XXe siècle*, La Nef, Paris, 1963.

Motret: *Essai d'explication de deux quatrains de Nostradamus*, Nevers, 1806.

Mouan, L: 'Aperçus littéraires sur César Nostradamus et ses lettres inédites à Peiresc', Mémoires de l'Académie, vol. 10, Aix, 1873. (BMA)

Moult, Thomas-Joseph: *Prophéties perpétuelles, très anciennes et très certaines*, seventeenth-century almanac.

Prophéties perpétuelles, Ed. des Cahiers astrologiques, Nice, 1941.

Moura, Jean, and Louvet, Paul: *La vie de Nostradamus*, Gallimard, Paris, 1930.

Muraise, Eric: *Du Roy perdu à Louis XVII*, Julliard, Paris.

Saint-Rémy de Provence et les secrets de Nostradamus, Julliard, Paris, 1969.

Histoire et Légende du grand Monarque, 'Les Chemins de l'Impossible', Albin Michel, Paris, 1975.

Necroman, Don: *Comment lire les Prophéties de Nostradamus*, Ed. Maurice d'Hartoy, Paris, 1933.

Neyral, Georges: *La Vraie Vie de Michel de Nostredame*, Thesis, Toulouse, 1951.

Nicoullaud, Charles: *Nostradamus, ses prophéties*, Perrin et Cie, Paris, 1914.

Nostradamus, César: *Poésies*, Colomiez, Toulouse, 1606–8.

L'Entrée de la reine Marie de Médicis en sa ville de Salon, Jean Tholoson, Aix-en-Provence, 1602.

Histoire et Chroniques de Provence, Simon Rigaud, Lyon, 1614.

Nostradamus, Michel: *Les Prophéties de M. Michel Nostradamus:* Principal Editions:

    Macé Bonhomme, Lyon, 1555;
    Antoine du Rosne, Lyon, 1557–58;
    Barbe Régnault, Paris, 1560;
    Pierre Rigaud, Lyon, 1566;
    Benoist Rigaud, Lyon, 1568; in 8. *B.U. Montepellier*, no. 48340.
    Charles Roger, Paris, 1569;
    Pierre Meunier, Paris, 1589;
    Jean Poyet, Lyon, 1600 (BN);
    Benoist Rigaud, Lyon, 1605;
    Pierre Rigaud, Lyon, 1605 (BN);
    Pierre Rigaud, Lyon, 1610 (BN), 1649;
    Claude La Rivière, Lyon, 1611;
    Vincent Sève, Beaucaire, 1610;
    Pierre Chevillot, Troyes, 1611;
    Simon Rigaud, Lyon, 1644;

Pierre de Ruau, Troyes, 1649 (BN);

Winckermans, Amsterdam, 1657;

Jean Balam, Lyons, 1665;

Jean Ribon, vis-à-vis la Sainte Chapelle à l'image Saint Louis, Paris, 1669;

Jean Huguetan, Lyon (17th century);

Jean Ianson, Amsterdam, 1668;

Jean Besongne, Rouen, 1681;

Besson, Lyon, 1691;

Jean Viret, Lyon, 1697 (BML);

Lambert-Gentot, *Nouvelles et Curieuses prédictions de M. Nostradamus, pour sept ans depuis l'année 1818 jusqu'à l'année 1824*, Lyon, 1818.

Landriot, Riom, no date (19th century);

Facsimiles of the 1611 Chevillot edition by Delarue, Paris, and of the 1668 Amsterdam edition by Ed. Adyar, Paris 1936.

Prognostication nouvelle et prédiction portenteuse pour l'an 1555 composées par Maistre M. Nostradamus, Jean Brotot, Lyon.

Démonstration d'une comette, Jean Marcorelle, Lyon, 1571 (BN)

Prognostication et prédiction des quatre temps pour 1572, Melchior   Arnoullet, Lyon, 1572. (BN)

Prophéties par l'Astrologue du Très Chrétien Roy de France et de Madame la Duchesse de Savoye, F. Arnoullet, Lyon, 1572. (BN)

Nostradamus, Michel: *Lettre de Maistre Michel Nostradamus de Salon-de-Craux-en-Provence à la Royne, mère du Roy*, Benoist Rigaud, Lyon, 1566.

Almanach pour l'an 1573 avec les présages, Pierre Roux, Avignon, 1562.

Prophétie ou Révolution merveilleuse des 4 saisons de l'an, Michel Jove, Lyon, 1567.

Traité de fardements et confitures, Antoine Volant, Lyon, 1555.

Paraphrase de C. Galen, trans. by Nostradamus, Antoine du Rosne, *Excellent et très utile opuscule de plusieurs exquises receptes*, Benoist Rigaud, Lyon, 1572. Lyon, 1557.

Almanach pour l'an 1567, Benoist Odo, Lyon.

La Grant Pronostication nouvelle avec la déclaration ample de 1559, Jean Brotot, Lyon, 1558.

Prophéties sur Lyon, La France et le monde entier dans les premières années du XXe siècle, 5 booklets, Lyon, P. Bousset & M. Paquet, 1907, 1909.

Almanach des prophéties, P. N. Jausserand, Lyon, 1871–72.

Les Merveilleuses Centuries et Prophéties de Nostradamus, colour illustrations by Jean Gradassi, Ed. André Virel, Ed. Artisanales SEFER, 880 copies, Nice, 1961.

Les Prophéties de Nostradamus (complete), Club des Champs Elysées, Ed. Baudelaire, Paris, 1967.

Prophéties nouvelles de Michel Nostradamus trouvées dans sa tombe au moment de l'ouverture dans l'église des Cordeliers de salon pour 1820, 1821, 1822, 1823, 1824, 1825 et 1826, A Toulon de l'Imprimerie de Calmen, imprimeur du Roi, 11, rue d'Angoulême.

Les Prophéties de Nostradamus (complete), Les Cent un chefs d'oeuvre du Génie Humain, Prodifu, 5, rue du Cog Héron, 75001 Paris.

Les Prophéties de Nostradamus, pub. by the author, Marc Billerey, Mallefougasse (Alpes de Provence), 1973.

Undated edns (16th and 17th centuries): Antoine Baudraud et Pierre André, Lyon.

Nostredame, Jean de: *Les Vies des plus célèbres et anciens poètes provençaux qui ont fleuri du temps des comtes de Provence*, Basile Bouquet, Lyon, 1575.

Novaye, Baron de: *Aujourd'hui et demain*, Paris, 1905.

Pagliani, Coraddo: 'Di Nostradamus e idi sue una poco nota iscrizione Liminare torinen', in *Della Rassegna mensile Muncipale*, no. 1, Turin, 1934.

Parisot, F.: *Le Grand Avènement précédé d'un grand prodige*, typographie des Célestins, Bar-le-Duc, 1873.

Parker, Eugène: *La Légende de Nostradamus et sa vie réelle*, Paris, 1923.

Patrian, Carlo: *Nostradamus, le Profezie*, Edizioni Méditerranée, Via Flaminia, Rome, 1978.

Pelaprat, Jean Marie: 'Varennes et 1792, sauvent Nostradamus', *Historia*, no. 397(2), *Voyance et Prophéties*, Ed. Tallendier, Paris.

Pichon, Jean-Charles: *Nostradamus et le Secret des temps*, Les Productions de Paris, 1959.

Nostradamus en clair, R. Laffont, Paris, 1970.

Le Royaume et les Prophètes, R. Laffont, 1963.

Piobb, P. V.: Facsimile of Amsterdam edn, Adyar, Paris, 1936.

Le Sort de l'Europe d'après la célèbre Prophétie des papes de Saint-Malachie, accompagnée de la Prophétie d'Orval et de toutes dernières indications de Nostradamus, Dangles, Paris, 1939.

Privat, Maurice: *1938, année de relèvement*.

1938, année d'échéance.

1939, année de reprise, Editions Médicis, Paris, 1938.

Demain, la guerre.

1940, prédictions mondiales, année de grandeur française, Editions Médicis, Paris.

Putzien, Rudolf: *Friede unter Völkern? Die Weissagungen des M. Nostradamus und ihre Bedeutung für Atomzeitaler*, Drei Eichen Verlag, H. Kissener, Munich, 1958.

Reed, Clarence: *Great Prophecies about the war*, Faber & Faber, London, 1941.

Reynaud, Jean-Lucien: *Nostradamus n'a pas menti*, lecture, Ville d'Avray, 1948.

Nostradamus délié, Ville d'Avray, 1949.

Reynaud-Plense: *Les Vraies Prophéties de Nostradamus*, Salon, 1939.

Robb, Steward: *Nostradamus on Napoleon*, Oracle Press, New York, 1961.

Nostradamus on Napoleon, Hitler and the present crisis, Scribner's, New York, 1941.

Prophecies on world events by Nostradamus, New York, 1961.

Robert, Henry: *The Complete Prophecies of Nostradamus*, Ed. H. Robert, Great Neck, New York, 1971. Japanese trans. by Kasuko Daijyo with Hidéo Uchida, Ed. Tama, Tokyo, 1975.

Rochetaille, P.: *Prophéties de Nostradamus. The key to the 'Centuries', with special reference to the history of the Third Republic*, Adyar, 1939.

Roisin, Michel de: 'Ulrich de Mayence, maître de Nostradamus', *Aesculape*, no. 5, 1969, 52nd year.
'Plus forte que Nostradamus: Ulrich de Mayence', *Constellation*, no. 199, November 1964.
Rollet, Pierre: *Interprétation des Hiéroglyphes de Horapollo*, Ramoun Bérenguié, Aix-en-Provence, 1968.
Roudene, Alex: *Les Prophéties, vérité ou mensonge*, Mondes Magiques series, Ed. de l'Athanor, Paris, 1976.
Rouellond de la Rouellondière de Chollet: *La Prophétie de Rouellond, Manuscrit du XVIe siècle*, Victor Pipeau, Beauvais, 1861.
Rouvier, Camille: *Nostradamus*, Marseille, La Savoisienne, 1861.
Ruir, Emile: *Le Grand Carnage d'après les prophéties de Nostradamus de 1938 à 1947*, Ed. Médicis, Paris, 1938.
L'Ecroulement de l'Europe, d'après les prophéties de Nostradamus, Paris. 1939.
Ruir, Emile: *Nostradamus, ses Prophéties, 1948–2023*, Paris, 1948.
Nostradamus. Les Proches et Derniers Evénements, Ed. Médicis, Paris, 1953.
Ruzo, Daniel: *Les Derniers Jours de l'Apocalypse*, Payot, 1973.
Los ultimos dias del apocalipsis, Michel Shultz, Mexico.
Sede, Gérard de: *Les Secrets de Nostradamus*, Julliard, Paris, 1969.
Spica-Capella: *La Clef des prédictions nostradamiques*, Ed. des soirées astrologiques, 1941.
Tamizey de Larroque: *Les Correspondants de Pieresc, César Nostradamus*, unpublished letters from Salon to Peiresc, 1628–29, Typographie Marius Olive, Marseille, 1880.
Tarade, Guy: 'La Clef des centuries de Nostradamus', *Pégase*, no. 3, 1974.
Les Dernières Prophéties pour l'Occident, 'Les Enigmes de l'Univers' series, Robert Laffont, Paris, 1979.
Torne-Chavigny, H.: Reissue of the *Prophecies of Nostradamus*, 1862 edition, enlarged in 1872.
Prospectus: interprétation de 30 quatrains, 1860.
L'Histoire prédite et jugée par Nostradamus, 3 vol., Bordeaux, 1860.
Affiches: tableau de l'histoire prédite et jugée, 1862.
Prospectus des lettres du grande prophète: interprétation de 20 quatrains.
Les lettres du grand prophète.
Henri V à Anvers.
Nostradamus et l'astrologie.
Les Blancs et les rouges.
La Salette et Lourdes.
La mort de Napoléon III.
MacMahon et Napoléon IV.
Le roy blanc et la fusion.
Portraits prophétiques d'après Nostradamus.
Prophéties dites d'Olivarius et d'Orval.
L'Apocalypse interprétée par Nostradamus, 1872.
Almanach du grand prophète Nostradamus pour 1873.
Nostradamus éclairci ou Nostradamus devant monseigneur Dupanloup, Saint-Denis-du-Pin, 1874.

Ce qui sera d'après le grand prophète Nostradamus, followed by *Almanach pour 1878*.

Influence de Nostradamus dans le gouvernement de la France, 1878.

Concordance de Nostradamus avec l'Apocalypse, Veuve Dupuy, Bordeaux, 1861.

Touchard, Michel: *Nostradamus*, Grasset, 1972
  'Histoire des personnages mystérieux et des sociétiés secrètes' series, Ed. Celt, Paris, 1972.

Touchard, Michel: 'Les Prophéties de Michel Nostradamus. Le rêve fou', *Historia*, no. 34, 1974.

Tronc de Condoulet: *Abrégé de la vie de Nostradamus* followed by *Nouvelle découverte de ses quatrains*, J. Adibert, Aix-en-Provence. (BMA)

Van Gerdinge, René: 'Le Nez de Cléopâtre', *Messidor*, no. 29, Montfavet, Vaucluse.

Verdier, du: *Les Vertus de notre maistre Nostradamus*, Geneva, 1562.

Viaud, Jean: '1999, Un tournant dans l'histoire des hommes', *Constellation*, no. 166, Feb. 1962.

Vidél, Laurent: *Déclaration des abus, ignorances et séditions de Michel Nostradamus*, Avignon, 1558.

Vignois, Elisée du: *Notre Histoire racontée à l'avance par Nostradamus*, Paris, 1910.

L'Apocalypse, interprète de la Révolution, d'après Nostradamus, Noyon, 1911.

Vogel, Cyrille: *Saint Césaire d'Arles*, 1937.

Voldben, A.: *After Nostradamus*, Neville Spearman, London, 1973.

Ward, Charles A.: *Oracles of Nostradamus*, London, 1891.

Willoquet, Gaston: *La Vérité sur Nostradamus*, Ed. Traditionelles, Paris, 1967.

Winckermans: *Editions des Centuries*, Amsterdam, 1657.

Woolf, H. I.: *Nostradamus*, London, 1944.

Yram: *Prophéties connues et prédictions inédites*, Preface by Papus, l'Edition d'Art, Paris.

Zevaco, Michel: *Nostradamus* (novel), Fayard, 1909, Livre de Poche, no. 3306.

Table of Quatrains, Sextains and Prophecies

In the following pages the reader will find cross-references to all the quatrains, sextains and prophecies which appear in Volumes 1 and 2. Page numbers which refer to the latter are in italics.

The centuries run chronologically – in roman figures – along the top row, the years in the first column, and the page references to the quatrains, sextains and prophecies appear at the appropriate point in the grid itself.

	I	II	III	IV	V	VI	VII	VIII	IX	X	XI	XII	S	P
1	1	311	347/55			405							*116*	
2	2	52	*131*	112				272	243					43
3	286	337	*142*		160				169	279			362	
4	429		*153*		213	363/29	*142*	409					400	356
5	320		266	*148*	207	*122*		414	99	368				
6	157	358	*104*		407	283	319	355	378				30	
7	366	421				390		359		162			*125*	
8	*97*		200	16	362								331	370
9	*287/38*		241	354		109	*86*	*145*	381				56	
10	*126*		*127*	406	154	427	392	359	404	421				407
11	*114*	131		71	*150*	18		85	62	406				305
12	95	*139*	291	185	335	*102*	403	156		277				308
13	*107*		130	389		171	94 (xxvii)			104				
14	190			400	289			267					227	
15	170	284	44		280		*100*	327					413	385
16				168	337			269/40	199					
17	*119*		431		367			345	222	63				119
18	332	373	183	28				408	35	22				
19	*124*	249				202	165	76						
20		*103*	*83*		84				60					
21				394		341		319	73	259			226	*151*
22		*135*		123		297	281	381		*89*				
23	128		330	399	305	267	58	58		238				
24	*96*	*129*			144		396		66	125	379			
25		173	105		429	91	186						228	
26		353	269		191	86	103	37		31				330
27		*132*	287/39	273	369	*137*		221		397			306	

	P
101	295
102	
103	
104	
105	
106	
107	
108	
109	
110	
111	
112	
113	
114	
115	
116	
117	
118	
119	
120	
121	
122	
123	
124	*151*
125	304
126	
127	*139*

	I	II	III	IV	V	VI	VII	VIII	IX	X	XI	XII	S	P
28	325	418	153	46		389		266	335					
29	237	419			89		3		29	274			416	316
30		325	17		349	217			314				410	*138*
31	*147*		376			244	166		*112*	328/41			256	342
32	393	312		239		137				377				371
33			233	307	72			87	397	324				
34	209	289/52	77	402		363		276	55				426	348
35	5 (xxix)	275	204	132			268		136				257	
36		107		118		340					11			
37			172	350			431	311	383	387				
38		248		336		93	151	392		351				398
39	146	*95*	82	372	159		*99*						417	*136*
40	193	264/54		298						75			390	428
41	349	280					*153*	422	401				102	271
42			420	354	158	285		147	387					
43		281	117	113	364/31					48			34	
44	430	174	*108*	284	369	371		*147*	357	338			*130*	413
45			379	333	175					25			*134*	
46	273	265	361		299/49			272	380	96		265	303	
47	194	282	242		338									
48	367/33			318				*140*		198				
49	*149*	192	218	62	*92*	340		372	40	352				
50	*143*		164	373	376				425				308	293
51	427		19		384	64		326	383	179				
52		*143*				177		393	262	187		7	15	293
53		45	215			350		161	223				220	
54	148		*144*	101	425			411	235				230	292

	P
128	
129	*146*
130	
131	
132	
133	
134	
135	
136	
137	
138	
139	
140	
141	9

	I	II	III	IV	V	VI	VII	VIII	IX	X	XI	XII	S	P
55			20		427	*111*		*106*	184	433			67	
56	424				211	322						265	416/50	
57	61	50	195		275	76		108					97	295
58	134	65	203	343		411			57	370			*146*	
59		348	252	236				262			270/56			
60	80	291/57	288	21	100	33		395	313	290				315
61	90		288	240	386			391	10					
62	47	283	323	6	312	27		282		141				188
63	*123*		*115*	79	231	53			322					
64		358	13	149		263			323	245				
65	*94*	307		182				219		270	346			
66			70							422				
67		135	205			225		*93*						
68		309	144	290	402				278					300
69	432	145								329	356			
70	258		309	121	385/43	401		260						
71	*141*		310		360			28	384					
72	343	342		*135*				341	382	428				
73	331			154	306/53		110	365	405	*150*				
74	98	*140*		321	408	366				154/34				
75	115		111	129		14			140	425				297
76	81	126	206		395				224					396
77	114	181		412					423					
78	229	310	332			412			*88*					
79	380	409	378		116	353				415				
80	347			216	375	423		78						
81		374			415	355		246						

	I	II	III	IV	V	VI	VII	VIII	IX	X	XI	XII	S	P
82	334		318	333	180									
83							315		*136*					*152*
84		313	364		419	208								
85			324		317	336		122	274					
86	68	292		403				346	24	326				
87			38		178					410				
88	133	303	344	8				20		344				294
89	*118*		138	42	*84*				151	39				189
90	345	250	327/42	352	142	210			*87*					
91	264/60	328												
92	269		321		211	365				357				
93	*138*	432	394/31		*152*			298	398					
94	285	317		320	334			299/48	214					
95	415	286	368	377	*109*	176			234	375				
96		351		386	278/45	361		254						
97		277/46	253			302		*101*		316				
98	133	69	18		302	49	279							296
99	404	106	360	*90*	231			417	271	430				294
100				420					388	196